A Buddhist Spectrum

A Buddhist Spectrum

Contributions to Buddhist-Christian Dialogue

by MARCO PALLIS

THE SEABURY PRESS · NEW YORK

1981
The Seabury Press
815 Second Avenue
New York, N.Y. 10017

Printed in the United States of America

Library of Congress Cataloging in Publication Data

Pallis, Marco, 1895-
    A Buddhist spectrum.

    1. Buddhism—Doctrines—Addresses, essays,
lectures.   I. Title.
BQ4165.P34   1981   294.3'4   80-26307
ISBN 0-8164-0493-3

Foreword

One of the most difficult things, when writing a book, is to find a good title, one which somehow expresses the nature of the work yet is neither academic-sounding, nor so picturesque as to mystify one's prospective readers, nor heavy-fisted nor complicated – there is no end to the traps into which a seeker of titles can fall.

In the present case I hope that a title has been found for a book which is not a consecutive treatise on Buddhism yet deals with a number of Buddhist themes of prime importance in such fashion as to make up a whole; between them these themes add up to a coherent view of the world and of a human destiny realisable in this world as seen through Buddhist eyes. Each colour of the spectrum is distinct and brilliant, yet they all tail into one another imperceptibly; in Pure Land Buddhist parlance, all these colours come together to form the halo of Amitabha Buddha, whose name means 'infinite light'; light, itself uncoloured yet including all possible colours, is Buddhahood's most characteristic symbol. The analogy between the spectrum and a series of separate but interdependent studies grouping themselves around a common idea should be clear enough.

Of the ten essays that have been brought together in this collection, some date back a considerable time, while others have been completed only recently. The fact that most of them were composed in answer to specific requests from other people will account for a certain amount of repetition affecting quotations and other illustrative features. This will not, I venture to hope, be regarded by readers as a drawback: the fact of meeting again something one has seen before can serve as a stimulus to the mind by intensifying the previous impression, and also to view the same material from different angles helps to illustrate the polyvalent character of the dharma the Lord Buddha revealed to us.

A word of explanation is owed to the reader in regard to two of these essays (III and VIII), of which the connection with Buddhism is admittedly not self-evident. The former was originally composed for reading before a predominantly Christian group, who doubtless expected a paper on a stock subject belonging to that Tibetan tradition with which the author's name had become associated; it occurred to me, however, that it might be more rewarding to tackle a subject which Christian minds notoriously have found troublesome, by applying to its discussion a characteristically Buddhist dialectical technique: Buddhism does indeed figure in that essay, but only incidentally along with other traditions. As for the eighth essay, its subject matter is inseparably linked to Christian motives, since musical polyphony has never found a place among the artistic resources of any Oriental religion. Its inclusion here can nevertheless be justified, if indirectly, by the fact that, but for an acquaintance with the teachings about *samsāra*, the existential round, as expounded by the Indian traditions, the hidden analogy with musical counterpoint could scarcely have come into my mind. My own lifelong experience in handling contrapuntal music made that analogy all the more telling.

A few special remarks about the next to last essay, the one on *anattā*, also seem called for. This is the most challenging subject I have ever tried to deal with and it was only after recurrent hesitations that I finally decided to make the attempt. From a Buddhist standpoint *anattā* constitutes a basic idea; it is in fact one of the features distinguishing Buddhism from its sister traditions in India and *a fortiori* from the Semitic forms of wisdom. In practice, *anattā* has been productive of much confusion among persons writing in European languages, whether as exponents or as critics of this doctrine; sectarian animus has also at times entered in to fog the issue still further. It would be rash for anyone to claim that he had produced an exhaustive explanation of this thorny subject; in fact what I have tried among other things to show is why such could never be the case; non-selfhood defends itself, as it were, against all attempts at a self-contained rationalisation. I can only express the hope that such thoughts on the subject as have been assembled in the pages of this book may be of some help, and not just one more hindrance, to the reader intent on penetrating the mystery for which the word *anattā* is meant to provide a key.

As for the tenth essay, this was sheer afterthought, provoked by my reading through a script by another author in which the subject of archetypes was brilliantly expounded while leaving certain portions of the field still fallow; this was precisely the part that I have felt moved to plough. The outcome was this essay. Moreover, I must confess that this subject as a whole was unfamiliar ground for me; to explore it was an effort, but one well worth making, if only because the archetypal principle is one which has a wide practical applicability irrespective of what religious path a man happens to be following or even if he still remains a seeker.

The word 'archetype' does not seem to date far back in time, perhaps no earlier than the Renaissance. The idea itself is not new, however; no religion can be without it, however this truth may be expressed. On reading my colleague's text I asked myself how this particular subject should be envisaged from a Buddhist point of view; this essay marks an attempt to answer that question. Christian sources have also been drawn on freely here; this is a case where two ways of treating the same theme will serve to reinforce each other, without raising any awkward questions.

M.P.

Note on transcription of foreign words

Though it has been common practice to italicise technical terms of foreign origin, this is apt to read tediously once those terms have become familiar by dint of repetition: words like samsāra, karma, dharma, nirvana, provide examples. For this reason such common words have here been italicised only in special cases. In the case of rarer words drawn from Sanskrit, Tibetan, Arabic, etc., the habit of using italics has been adhered to.

Contents

I

Living One's Karma

The conception of existence as *samsāra*, cosmic flux, together with its parallel conception of *karma*, 'concordant action and reaction' as the determinant of each being's part in that flux, is an essential feature of all the traditions directly or indirectly deriving from India. Though the subject is here being considered from a Buddhist angle, most of what will be said could apply to Hinduism equally well.

Let us first consider the Round of Existence through its symbolical representation, said to go back to the Buddha himself, as a circle subdivided into six sectors, each containing one of the typical classes of sentient beings. These sectors can be arranged in three pairs, as follows:

our world: (1) human (the central state); (2) animals
    (peripheral states)
supernal worlds: (3) gods, or *devas*; (4) titans, or *asuras*
infernal worlds: (5) tantalised ghosts, or *pretas*; (6) hells.

This symbolic scheme is familiar wherever the Buddhist tradition prevails.

Let us examine each of the six components in somewhat greater detail. Quite evidently, the human sector, which was mentioned first, has been given a disproportionate share in the whole if one considers it solely from the point of view of the number of beings concerned. Compared with the vast multiplicity of their non-human neighbours, men represent a very small number indeed, apart from the fact that they form but one species as compared with an immense variety extending to genera, families, and natural orders. The reason for this privileged treatment is twofold: first, being men ourselves, it is natural for us to single out for study our own kind and manner of existing; second, the human species is the chosen field of avataric embodiment, Buddhahood, and this, qualitatively speaking, entitles it to privileged consideration.

Passing to the animal sector, this contains a large number of different species situated at the same level of existence as man, but varying in respect of their nearness to, or remoteness from, the human position. It might then be asked: where do plants and minerals come in, since they do not seem to figure by name in any sector? The answer can only be that here one is not dealing with a chart of biological or geological statistics; one must not expect a meticulous consistency in regard to details. All the traditional picture of the Round is intended to do is to serve as a broadly sufficient guide to an understanding of the universe, one that is based, all along, on qualitative factors rather than on 'facts' or quantitative considerations such as enter into the purview of natural sciences in the usual sense of the word.

Regarded from the human point of view, the supernal states are those that in greater or lesser measure escape the physical and psychic limitations of our own state of existence. The two sectors grouped in the supernal class may, however, themselves include quite a number of different degrees that we, in our present state, are hardly concerned with. It is said of gods, or devas, that theirs is a state full of delights such as 'wishing trees' able to grant any boon at the mere thought, and other picturesque amenities of a similar kind; no pain can enter into this state while it lasts, which makes the moment of change when it strikes at long last all the more painful for the beings in question, as they suddenly wake up to the fact that their state of bliss is not eternal but remains subject to birth and death like every other existential state. As one Mongolian monk said to the writer: 'The long-lived gods are stupid.' Lulled into overconfidence by sheer absence of contrast in their present condition, they are wholly unprepared for the fatal moment when it comes, and they may sink as low as hell itself, a truly lamentable fate.

Not all the gods, however, display this lack of intelligence. Many of them play a creditable part in stories of the Buddha. Some, such as Vishnu's hawklike steed Garuda, are constant attendants on the Buddha's person, whose canopy they provide; others again, and especially Brahmā, king of the devas, after the Buddha's enlightenment persuade him to preach the doctrine lest the world be utterly lost. This overcoming of the Buddha's 'reluctance' at the instance of the gods features in the history of every teaching Buddha and is meant to convey symbolically that the knowledge possessed by an enlightened one is so profound as to be virtually incommunicable to men in their present state of ignorance. The Buddha, however, consents to teach, thus showing that, ignorance notwithstanding, the Light is not unattainable. For this we have to thank the persuasion of the gods.

Titans, or *asuras*, for their part, though superior to men in virtue of their possession of various powers, are always represented as contentious beings, full of envy for the gods and their felicity and ever plotting to dethrone them. Typically they are beings who through 'austerities', intense work carried out in various fields, have been enabled to extend their own natural faculties to the point of threatening heaven itself. Sometimes titanic ambition even wears an altruistic mask, as when Prometheus stole the fire from the gods in order to bestow it on mankind, thus exposing the latter to the consequences of his own act of profanation. It is typical of an asuric or Promethean temperament to promote recklessly the use of abnormal powers from every kind of motive except the essential one, the one that could lead a being to Buddhahood. Lacking this motive, it lacks all; such is the asuric sign in beings.

The two infernal sectors of our symbolism, the land of tantalised ghosts (*pretas*) and the hells, are places whence joy and comfort are entirely banished. The first-named is a realm wherein reigns the most intense feeling of want, an insatiable hunger and thirst. *Pretas* are pictured as having huge, inflated bellies and pinpoint mouths, so that enough nourishment can never find its way through the tiny inlet to meet the excessive cravings of the belly, and thus the being remains in a constant state of misery, which only a change of state may eventually relieve, could he but awaken to this possibility. The hells, on the other hand, more or less explain themselves: they are places of sheer expiation, hot or cold according to the nature of the offences committed (or opportunities disregarded) in the course of previous life. In this respect they hardly differ from the conception of hell as found in the Semitic religions except in matters of detail and, more especially, in the absence of any perfunctory attribution of 'eternity' such as does not belong anywhere in the Round.

3

This last is the most important point to grasp. The keynote of *samsāra* is *impermanence*, the primary theme to meditate upon for every Buddhist. All that the world's flow brings into being is unstable. This is true of heavens or hells, happier states as well as more unhappy; the former admit of no complacency, the latter are never entirely without hope. For everything, in the fullness of becoming, when its particular possibilities have spent themselves, must change to something else. This is the universal law of existence in the Round.

The number and variety of beings extant in the universe is incalculable. The same holds for world systems; they are indefinite both in their incidence and in the variety of conditions to which each world system is subject. But, whatever may be the conditions governing a given world, the sixfold grouping can still be applied to it, with suitable allowance made for differences of detail. Thus every world must have its 'central' or 'axial' state which, by analogy with our world, may well be called human; just as there will also exist superior and inferior states classifiable as such from the standpoint of that state that provides the median term.

The essential characteristics of each world are integrally reflected in the being that is central to that world and, in a more or less fragmentary manner, in the various beings occupying peripheral positions. The central state, being a totality in its own order, constitutes something like an autonomous world of its own, a microcosm, and this is the case with man in our world system. Knowing the state of man at a particular time, one can almost say one knows the state of the world, so closely are the two interests bound together. A transposition of the sixfold symbolism from the greater world in all its extension to the human microcosm follows logically from this interrelationship; thus certain properties of human nature can be said to correspond to certain classes of beings, in the sense that, in proportion as a man identifies himself with such a property rather than with such another, he will display, in his human life, something of the character of one or other of the non-human classes. To give one instance, it is easy to recognise the type conforming as nearly as possible to a state of 'human animality', that of men regarded chiefly in the mass as feeders and reproducers in a quantitative sense; needless to say, no disparagement of animals is intended by the above allusion, for animals and plants in a state of nature live out their karma with sure instinct and exhibit qualities of dignity and beauty that man, for his part, can emulate only by remaining faithful to his own vocation, which is of another order just because of his central position in the world.

To take another example, modern 'economic man' oscillates between the animal and *preta* types, the latter being the one that is most consonant with his professed ideal of an indefinitely expanding production and of a so-called high standard of living. A vast machine of propaganda exists for the sole purpose of exacerbating an appetite for possessions, with the proviso, however, that the happiness these are supposed to procure must never be quite reached, for if man rested satisfied at any point the wheels would stop going round there and then, and this would mean economic ruin, so inextricably have the two motives been geared to one another. Therefore man must keep on being tantalised into fresh desires – a far cry from Buddhism.

If this be not a picture of a Pretaland, it is the next best thing to one. And to what kind of rebirth are men schooled in this way likely to attain? Might it be to rebirth as *pretas* perhaps?

As for the hells, they are surely discernible among those dark reservoirs below the level of human consciousness wherein our psychologists so often like to fish. Sometimes their contents also overflow: an utterly subhuman type is not uncommon in our midst, even without mentioning what he himself calls art, a devilish appliance in its way. Naturally, one has been referring to extremes. The purer types are relatively rare; mostly one has to do with various blends and hybrids.

There is one other kind of man, however, the one who alone is able to realise the plenitude of the human possibility, and this is the man who identifies himself, in intention and practice, not with some samsarically conditioned human faculty, but with the axis of the human microcosm itself, the thread of Buddha-nature passing through the heart of every being, every world. For peripheral beings this identification can only be indirect and eminently passive; but with man, because he is an axial being by definition, this can also take place in active mode, without restriction of scope or finality. This, in fact, is the possibility of full awakening, Buddha-hood, and justifies the statement, found in the Semitic scriptures, that man has been made 'in the divine image'. Whether we call man 'theomorphic' or 'buddhamorphic', it makes little difference in this context.

Lastly, let us return to the traditional portrayal of the Round of Existence, as originally described, in order to point out that, like every true symbolism, it derives from the nature of things and not from some arbitrary contrivance of the human mind as if it were just a poetic allegory. Its purpose is to serve as a key to a heightened awareness; it has no other use.

A symbolical classification like the present one is not meant to be read in the sense of a compact formula: it has to be freely interpreted and intelligently applied, for *samsāra* as such is *indefinite*, it does not admit of systematisation. The sutras in fact describe it as 'without beginning' (i.e. undefined in terms of origin) but as 'having an end' (in deliverance, Nirvana) – a paradoxical description since, metaphysically speaking, what has no beginning cannot have an end either, and vice versa. One can compare with this the similar (but inverse) Christian paradox of a world 'with beginning' (in creation) yet able to become 'world without end' (by salvation through Christ).

In both the above cases the object is to communicate a saving truth, not a nicely rounded-off philosophical thesis – hence an apparent disregard of logic.

We said at the outset that in samsāra the determinant of any coming into being or 'birth' is antecedent action, with its consequent reaction. This is the doctrine of *karma* and its fruits, which, ripening in their season as results, are fated in their turn to become causes containing, as they do, the seeds of further becoming. The continual intercrossing of numberless strands of causality goes to make up the skein of samsāra; the conception is dynamic, a continual passage from state to state, with each birth marking a death to some preceding state and each death marking a fresh birth and so on indefinitely.

Since everything is in a state of ceaseless flux, any event or object one chooses to observe has to be abstracted from the whole process in a more or less arbitrary manner, with the result that whatever one observes will necessarily have a certain character of ambiguity: both the object itself and the observing subject are changing all the time, which means that any judgement passed on the basis of an empirical examination of objects found in the world will remain approximate, provisional, relative, fluid, and ambivalent. The empirical approach precludes any conclusion qualifiable as 'exact' and 'complete'.

6

Having said this much, it is necessary also to mention the complementary aspect of the same doctrine, lest one be led unconsciously into a relativism that will itself assume a quasi-absolute character, to the point of doing away with all idea of truth itself; in these days of far-fetched and one-sided subjectivism, a dissolution of all objective values and criteria in a kind of psychoanalytical penumbra is a real danger and must be guarded against. A judgement is inadequate insofar as it claims to judge the whole absolutely from a particular standpoint likewise treated as absolute; this is the error of 'dogmatism', that is, of an abusive stretching of relative formulations that are true as far as they go. A judgement is valid, however, insofar as, starting out from criteria duly recognised to be relative, it judges a phenomenon whose relative limits are likewise recognised. Given that one is vigilantly heedful of these conditions, a judgement can be perfectly exact, to the point of being called 'relatively absolute' within its proper context.

A Buddha is called an awakened one just because his knowledge owes nothing to the world or to the empirical ego that jointly provided the focus of his previous dreaming. When a man wakes from sleep, we do not say he is someone else, despite an apparent change in the nature of his consciousness; this analogy gives an inkling of the passage from the state of an ignorant being to Buddhahood. Knowledge is only possible inasmuch as the 'eye of *bodhi*' (the pure intellect), in the subject, perceives, in the object, the 'bodhic message' (i.e. its symbolism). When these two coincide, there is instant awareness – eternal awareness, as one might say, inasmuch as what pertains to bodhi belongs *per se* to the intemporal and the changeless. The awakening to knowledge, at any degree, is like the flashpoint reached by the rubbing together of two sticks; the *satori* of Zen is of this nature. Were things otherwise, enlightenment would not be a possibility for beings.

In samsāra it is evident that one can only judge fragments from standpoints no less fragmentary; in nirvana such a question does not arise. Awareness of samsaric differences and our own response to them on the strength of that awareness detracts in no wise from the intrinsic reality of phenomena considered as a whole. Their totality then brings us back to samsāra as such, and this, in essence, brings us back to nirvana. Here we meet a basic Buddhist principle, namely that he who really understands samsāra or karma, which comes to the same, understands nirvana. To see a single grain of dust in full awareness is to see the universe; no more is needed for enlightenment, wherein absolute and relative knowledge, the Buddha's two modes of truth, make but one.

What one always needs to bear in mind is that the world with its phenomena amounts to a play of compensations in such fashion that, though every part is ever shifting and therefore out of balance and ungraspable in itself, yet the whole, qua whole, remains unchanged across all its vicissitudes, as does the ocean in spite of its many waves and currents. If we try to define one of those waves in fixed terms, it will elude us, yet each reveals the unchanging in its own way. Hence the statement that a Buddha is to be found in every drop of water, every grain of sand.

This non-graspable nature of all things in existence is what has given rise, in the Buddhist spiritual economy, to another basic idea, one that people have found especially difficult to understand, namely the idea of *anattā*, 'non-selfhood', as applying to beings at all levels and to the manifested universe itself.

We have seen that the basic 'notes' of existence are relativity, impermanence, and becoming, to which we must add 'suffering', which is the characteristic that expresses the preceding three in the consciousness of beings. Universal possibility being unique, it excludes repetition in existence. In the cosmos there can be likeness or analogy at every degree but never absolute identity or selfhood.

What does the word 'selfhood' really convey to our minds? It conveys unequivocal purity, total non-admixture. A substance can be called pure only when it is nothing else but itself, being free from any trace of 'otherness'. Being such, it carries no incentive to change. It is the ambivalent character of the relative that is the root of change, for where there is more than one pole of attraction (or repulsion) there instability will prevail in some degree. What is wholly free from internal tensions cannot die, for what should there be to make it die? Whatever is liable to death, therefore, implies a dualism, the presence of forces pulling different ways, a composition of things partly incompatible, and this, by definition, is other than selfhood. It is the sharpening, in the course of becoming, of its internal contradictions that eventually causes a thing to fall apart, at the moment we call death.

When we are led to fix our attention, not on the process of becoming as a whole, but on an abstracted part of it (which may be our own person or any other thing), we are thereby easily led into attributing to that thing a fixed character. The same applies to a situation or an act when so regarded for its own sake. This is the error of *false attribution*, the congenital ignorance attaching to all extant beings as such. The specifically Buddhist doctrine of *anattā* is a way of dispelling this ignorance.

Let us now pass over to the more detailed consideration of karma, the impelling force behind every rebirth or redeath, that is to say *action* taken in the broadest sense of the word (including its negative aspect, *omission*) together with its inseparable accompaniment, the reaction it inescapably provokes, the two being strictly proportioned to one another. The physical principle that action and reaction are equal and opposite is but one example of this universal cosmic dispensation.

Now, like everything else the mind is concerned with, this law of karma were best contemplated in a purely detached, impersonal way, as if we ourselves were standing outside the Round of Existence and looking at it from the vantage point of a lofty and distant peak. But in point of fact such is not the case. We are deeply involved at every moment of our earthly sojourn and consequently, insofar as we feel ourselves to be 'this person so-and-so' distinct from all the beings who, for us, fall under the collective heading of 'other', we cannot help assessing this cosmic play going on all around us in terms of plus or minus, profit or loss, pleasure or pain, 'good' or 'evil', as we call them. This it is that accounts for the fact that in religious life karma has been explained, more often than not, in terms of moral sanction, as reward for good deeds and punishment for ill deeds, and this is how the matter is regarded, almost always, by the popular mind.

Such a view is not in itself false; indeed it can be salutary. The only falseness is if one imagines this to be the whole story, the first and last word to be said on the subject. A full awareness of the implications of karma will carry one outside the circle of moral alternatives and of the attachments that a personally biased view inevitably will foster in the long run; but nevertheless, for the common run of mortals, the view of karma as *immanent justice*, in the moral sense, is not unwholesome, since it inclines a man at least to take the lessons of karma seriously and apply them in his day-to-day life. All ethical laws, in every religion, have this character; they are *upāyas*, 'means', far-reaching but still relative in scope, a fact that incidentally explains why the most hallowed of moral laws sometimes will not work, so that even in this sphere one must expect the occasional exception, if only 'to prove the rule'.

Immanent justice, in its fullest sense, is nothing else but the equilibrium of the universe, that state of balance between all the parts that the quivering scales express but do not visibly achieve; but here again we have come outside the moral perspective which, though includable in the general panorama of 'justice', no longer needs to be given privileged emphasis in view of a particular human interest.

It is a commonplace with Buddhist controversialists, out to criticise what they look on as the arbitrary explanations offered by the theistic religions, to argue that the doctrine of karma, by accounting for the apparent irregularities of fate in terms of antecedent action leading to present sanction, is 'more just' than other views relating to the same facts. It is well to point out that once such an argument becomes clothed in a moral form it becomes every bit as anthropomorphic as the teachings about 'the will of God' in relation to sin current in the Christian and kindred religions. The use of this kind of language and all arguments taking this form can be justified empirically, as satisfying the need of certain minds and, if so, it is no small profit. However, any simplification of this kind must always be accounted an expression of 'popular apologetics' rather than of deep awareness of what really is at stake. It is nevertheless a mistake to laugh at such a view of things; if one is able to see the fallacy behind the argument, one is free to transcend it in deeper understanding of the same truth, without taking up a patronising attitude toward the simple souls for whom this argument has provided a stepping-stone in the way.

Speaking more generally, the important thing when comparing doctrines as propounded by different traditions is to find out, by an examination conducted with insight – scholarly scrupulousness in comparing the material is not by itself enough – whether the seeming divergences betray a genuine opposition or only a divergence of spiritual genius, since both things are possible. Every religion resorts to certain accommodations in the doctrinal field in order to bring various truths within the purview of an average mind; it is left to the saint and the sage to see beyond these somewhat garbled versions in order to find the truth they nevertheless convey in their own fashion. Here we see the difference between religion under its 'exoteric' aspect, adequate to a collective need, and under the aspect qualifiable as 'esoteric', where no such concessions have a place. This distinction rests not on a rigid compartmenting of religious truth but rather on the need for a graded approach to that same truth, the bright light of which has to be tempered to men's varying capacities of vision. The two broad categories we have mentioned explain themselves sufficiently in the light of this principle, which is an *upāya* of general applicability to every spiritual path.

An instance of how popularised interpretations can lead to a certain amount of doctrinal distortion is provided by current beliefs in Buddhist countries concerning the possibility of 'rebirth as a man'. People all too readily assume that a human rebirth, provided they keep leading fairly ethical lives (often at a lowish level), is there for the asking. I could mention several examples of this kind of attitude from my own experience, by no means all of them drawn from among the simple and uneducated. People find it easy to imagine that it is but a matter of a little careful moral accountancy on their part, and their next human life will be as good as assured. With these people 'merit', good karma, comes to be regarded wholly in a quantitative sense, rather as if it could be meted out by the pound, a matter of manipulating a neat double-column balance sheet in such a way as not to leave oneself too heavily in debt. They forget the common dictum about 'human birth hard to obtain' and the Buddha's parable about the purblind turtle swimming in a vast ocean where there is also a piece of floating wood with a hole in it. He estimated any particular being's chances of obtaining a human birth as about equal to the likelihood of that turtle pushing its head through that hole.

By this far-fetched parable he evidently wished to impress on people the extreme precariousness of the human chance, warning them thus against the folly of wasting a precious opportunity in trivial pursuits. In a world that likes to think of itself as 'progressive', how many people, I wonder, make even a slight attempt to follow this advice?

Let everyone only ask himself the question 'Do I give the Buddha and his teachings (or Christ and his teachings, for that matter), say, half an hour's worth of attention per day of my life?' and if the answer is in the negative, is it then reasonable to expect, under the law of karma, to receive another human chance in this or other worlds? And if one is prepared to give an honest answer to this question, one must surely go on to ask oneself another, namely 'Why then do I so unaccountably hang back?' The opportunity lies here and now, this is certain; what sense is there in banking on some dubious future, on the strength of a naive attempt to strike a bargain with God? – if we may here permit ourselves a turn of phrase that is not strictly Buddhist.

The essential thing to remember about the human state or any state describable as 'central' is that it marks the point where exit from the fatal round of birth and death is possible without the prior need to pass through another state of conditioned existence. The door is there, whereas if one has been born into some more peripheral situation it is indispensable, before one can aspire to deliverance, to gain a footing on the axis, in other words to find the way to a human birth. Once on the axis, the path lies open, trodden by all the Buddhas; what is essential is not merely to occupy one's human position passively, thanks to the karma that placed one there, but to realise it *actively*, and this is the express concern of a spiritual life.

If we pause to consider our present state of existence attentively, we will soon discover that it is, after all, not every man born who can be said to possess true humanity; we have already touched on this point when speaking of the human microcosm. In practice most human beings lead more or less subhuman lives, by which is meant not that they are all great criminals – the Macbeths and Iagos of this world are comparatively rare – but that so much of their time and attention goes in trivialities utterly incompatible with a human status; were life on earth fated to last a thousand years, they could hardly be more wasteful of it. Certainly, few escape this reproach altogether, even among those claiming some sort of religion for themselves. There is nothing more salutary than self-examination on this issue; a detailed diary if honestly kept would make cruel reading for many of us.

What everyone needs to remind himself of in the first place (if he gets so far) is that, before he can even begin to ascend the axial mountain that leads towards Buddhahood, he has first to become 'true man' (as Taoism puts it), which, in our world, is the station from which the mountain itself begins to rise; and that is why religion, in general, starts off by propounding the need for a purposeful life of virtue, because this chiefly is a means of regaining the missing human norm, the one we all bear in name but rarely possess in fact.

So far, karma has chiefly been considered under its cosmic aspect as the determinant, for beings, of their fate. Plainly, when taken in this sense, karma can be accepted only in passive mode, since the nature of a being's existence in a given world is something that being is impotent to alter, wish as he may; in this sense, 'the hairs of your head are all numbered'. There is, however, side by side with this involuntary and imposed passivity, a possibility of living the same karma in active mode – that is to say, mindfully and intelligently – and here the human will, which allows us to choose this second way or to neglect it, counts decisively, since, without its active concurrence, all we have to do is to let ourselves drift to and fro like logs floating on the surface of samsāra's swirling waters; but this attitude hardly befits those who, by virtue of their human quality, already stand at the wicket gate of freedom.

For a way to be justly describable as 'active' it must be clearly related, under the double heading of intention and method, to the promoting of enlightenment. A way that does not look beyond samsāra, even though some active elements may be called into play incidentally in the course of gaining merit, remains essentially passive in respect of its finality, and by this criterion it falls short.

For karma to be utilisable as an instrument to serve the greater purpose, a number of technical conditions have to be satisfied, three of which are of particular importance, so that they can fittingly provide the conclusion to this essay. The three are as follows. First, there must be conscious self-identification with one's karma. Second, there must be just discernment as to what really constitutes 'good karma'. Third, one's karma must be recognised as the determinant of vocation, of one's own specific dharma.

Let us take each of these points in order:

1 The basis of self-identification with one's karma is the clear recognition that it is essentially just – just in principle and just in the particular, including that particular we call 'myself'. Similarly one's future karma has to be accepted, as if by anticipation; one must expect to reap as one has sown and not otherwise.

What must be remembered at every turn is that karma is the expression of the inherent equilibrium of the universe, which is always present *in toto*, with every apparent disturbance of balance automatically entailing its compensating reaction whereby the total balance is maintained; karma is therefore not only just; it expresses the very principle of justice, which is *even balance*.

For man, an attitude of acceptance in the face of his state of existence, as determined by antecedent karma, as also in the face of the unavoidable happenings of his existence while that state lasts, the fruits of karma, is both realistic in itself and morally sound. This attitude has often been stigmatised as 'fatalistic', especially when displayed by Orientals, but the intended criticism starts out from a faulty premise, namely from a confusing of mere passivity versus one's fate with *resignation*, which is an intellectual attitude, active therefore and allied to detachment; it rests on an understanding of a real situation by a mind free from wishful thinking.

Fatalism, which also exists among men, can be imputed only where someone adopts a helpless attitude in respect of elements still indeterminate and therefore still offering openings for the free exercise of willing and acting in some degree or other. If, for instance, the house catches fire or if one's child is taken ill, these are results of karma and must, so far as that goes, be accepted; but there is no evidence to prove that standing by and letting the fire consume the house or failing to call in the doctor (whose existence in the neighbourhood, incidentally, is also a fruit of karma) is an already predestined fact, and it would be straining the doctrine of karma to hold back from an obviously reasonable, as well as possible, action on the strength of a pessimistically prejudged result. Lack of initiative and a spirit of resignation are two very different things.

Admittedly the kind of attitude we have been describing is sometimes to be found among simple people, especially in the East, so that the accusation of fatalism is not unjustified in some cases. Equally often, however, the attitude decried as fatalism is not such, but springs from true resignation in the face of unavoidable ills, in which case it is wholly justifiable and sane; just as, on the other hand, a congenital readiness of Western people to fight an apparently losing battle is often rewarded by an unexpected success and represents realism of another kind, namely a willingness to challenge fate as long as the least hope remains of altering a bad situation for the better. Each of the two attitudes has its proper place in human affairs, and each goes with its characteristic abuse;

between an unthinking fatalism and a tendency to kick obstinately against the pricks there is not much to choose.

The point to grasp is that though the dispensations of karma, once declared, have to be accepted for what they are, as inherently just – therefore also without resentment, which would in fact be futile – yet at the same time the use of such resources as lie to hand (also thanks to one's karma) is justified pending a final declaration of the result. Within these limits remedial action is in no wise opposed to resignation.

The all-important thing, however, when undertaking any action aimed at promoting human welfare, whether at an individual or a collective level, is not to lose sight of the essential truth of impermanence, as pertaining to the action itself and its eventual consequences. Whatever degree of success or non-success may appear to attach to the latter, this will never be definitive in either sense, such being precluded by the very nature of that samsaric process in which both action and its fruits appear but episodically. The pathetic hope, fostered by the mystique of 'progress', that by a successive accumulation of human contrivances samsāra itself will somehow be, if not abolished, permanently tilted in a comfortable direction is as incompatible with Buddhist realism as with historical probability. Among obstacles to enlightenment there can be none greater than to forget samsāra and our own inescapable place in it – in other words, to forget the first of the Four Noble Truths, enunciated by the Buddha, namely the necessary association of existence with suffering in some degree or other.

Though we have spoken at some length about acceptance of one's karma as marking an important stage, a full self-identification with it takes one much further. For such to be realised it is necessary to recognise what should be an obvious fact, though often over-looked, namely that a man *is* his karma in the sense that all the various elements that together have gone into the composition of his empirical personality, what he and others take for his 'self', are one and all products of karma, and so are the modifications through which that personality passes in the course of its becoming: family, possessions, occasional happenings, illness, old age, or what you will. Apart from these 'accidental' products of becoming, that personality would not exist, and when they fall apart it no longer is. Therefore there is a real identity between the process and the product, and once this is clearly recognised it should be possible to go a stage further and make friends with one's karma as Savitri made friends with Death when he came to fetch her husband and conquered him by so doing.

2   Now for our second question: What constitutes good karma?

An average layman would probably answer something like this: merit, good karma, accrues to him who leads an upright, pious life, keeping the precepts, showing compassion to fellow creatures of every kind, and contributing duly to the support of the sacred congregation, the Sangha; if the man is a monk, he may add one or two items to the list, but broadly speaking this is the answer one will get. If one also asks him what are the fruits of meritorious karma, he will probably say, 'A healthy and happy life, a painless death, with rebirth into a state of felicity among gods or the like, or else again as man.' Now, this kind of answer, which is conventional, though acceptable as far as it goes, hardly makes for a far-reaching aspiration. The attitude remains samsaric; there is no touch of Buddha-thinking here.

From one in whom 'the mind of bodhi' has begun to stir, be it ever so slightly, a different answer is required. Before he calls his karma 'good' or 'bad' he will want to know, above all, whether or not it places him in favourable circumstances for encompassing 'the one thing needful', as Christ described it; rewards for merit, assessable only according to the scale of samsaric values, hold little attraction for such a man. A beatitude minus the essential opportunity is not far from being, for him, a hell.

Once a man begins to hold such views, his valuation of things around him and also in the world at large cannot but change its emphasis, since it will be influenced, at every turn, by this paramount consideration: is this conducive to enlightenment, or is it not, and if it is, how far is it so? This thought becomes the touchstone of discernment in things great and small, and nothing will henceforth be immune from reappraisal in the light of it.

By this criterion an unschooled beggar woman in Tibet strong in the faith of Buddha has a more enviable lot than many an eminent professor in other lands whose obsessive pursuit of purely samsaric investigations constitutes an obstacle a hundred times more insurmountable than mere illiteracy and some degree of petty superstition could ever be for that poor woman. On balance, the illiteracy might even count as a gain, since it will have screened her mind effectively from the contagion of cheap literature – or rather would have done so had she been born in Europe, since in Tibet before the communist invasion such a thing as profane literature was unknown, all books being attached to the sacred interest in some degree or other. The same, of course, would apply in any fully traditional society, whether of East or West. As between that woman and the professor, her simple faith, however limited, must count as an elementary knowledge, where colossal erudition, directed, not to the centre but to numberless peripheral phenomena, must count as a peculiarly pretentious form of ignorance. Therefore rebirth as that beggar woman, for the professor, would spell almost unqualified gain; the reverse, for her, unqualified loss.

An English traveller was once asked by a Tibetan: 'What is the good of trying to suppress all superstitions, since, on a final count, whatever exists outside bodhi, outside enlightenment, and whatever does not lead there, is but superstition?' A Mongol also once asked the writer if it was true that the British, as he had been given to understand, were all completely without superstitions of the kind commonly to be found among the people of his own country. On being given a few instances of superstitions still current in Europe he said, with evident relief, 'Then there is hope for these people after all, since their mind is not completely closed [he might have said 'sterilized'] in respect of things that do not meet the eye.' The above examples, which can be varied in a hundred ways, should be sufficient to illustrate the principle at play.

People speak of prosperity as if they had a right to it regardless of their karma, and of adversity as if it were something in which they had no stake; but here again it is necessary to discriminate in the light of the respective karmic fruits. For the man of insight, a form of prosperity tending to increase distraction (though this does not always happen, of course) must be reckoned a drawback from the point of view of fruits, whereas an adversity that serves to open one's eyes must be accounted more of a boon than a punishment; merit might earn a blessed pain, where an unfavourable karma would place one in prosperity as a stage on the way to hell.

For instance, would the early Christian martyrs have been gainers if in place of the terrible suffering they were called upon to face they had been born, say, as prosperous businessmen in New York today? Was that monk who was murdered for refusing to preach against religion at the bidding of the communists, or was that humble retainer they also murdered because he persisted in denying that the feudal landowner he served had behaved oppressively, a victim of bad, or a gainer of good, karma? On a short view they both suffered; on a long view both earned the crown of martyrdom. It is for oneself to judge which is the overriding criterion in every such case. Remember that in samsāra there are no absolute categories; every criterion can be read two ways. That is why each case that crops up has to be settled on its merits, in reference to the one supreme interest; otherwise one's conclusions will remain both crude and dubious.

One other example drawn from a source very foreign to the Buddhist world will help to clinch the argument. I remember an occasion some years ago when I sat listening to Wagner's music-drama *Die Walküre*. It was the scene where Wotan, chief of the gods, is about to sentence his daughter, Brunhilde, the celestial warrior-maiden, to deprivation of her godhood for having disobeyed his command to side with Hunding, and in his person with the laws of conventional morality, against Siegmund, who here stands for the cause of spirit versus the letter and as the exception that proves the rule. This story was taken by Wagner from an ancient German myth, a symbolical narrative that is to say, and as such charged with a metaphysical message that the composer must have felt instinctively even if he did not consciously penetrate its every meaning.

The crux of the story is that Wotan, to punish his daughter, turns her into an ordinary woman; by this token, Brunhilde is caused to exchange a state which, though it bespeaks superior powers, remains peripheral, in favour of the human state, which is central. Thus the seeming punishment becomes a real reward. As a further result, according to the myth, Brunhilde, now a woman, becomes the spouse of Siegfried, type of the Solar Hero – and let us not forget that traditionally 'solarity' is an attribute of the Buddha himself. If we translate the episode into Buddhist terms, Brunhilde's good karma, due to her having shown true discernment when faced with a crucial choice, won her a place on the axis of deliverance. This is the essential point; the 'punishment' is only incidental. This all came to me in a flash, as I sat under the spell of that glorious music, which thus served as an *upāya*, as a catalyst of wisdom hidden in the old German and Scandinavian mythology, which otherwise I might never have discovered for myself.

3 Third and last is karma as determinant of a man's vocation, of his own specific dharma:

We said, when discussing the first of our three headings, that a man *is* his karma inasmuch as he owes to it all the various elements of which his human personality is compounded, nothing being found there that he can call his own in the sense of a personal constant or selfhood.

Now, what is received through one's karma is necessarily delimited; it includes certain elements and excludes others, and these between them mark the positive and negative boundaries of the personality concerned. By the same token one is shown what possibilities of action lie open to one – as also of thought, since this is activity of a kind and limited in its own way. The things one lacks cannot be utilised; each man must work with the tools, mental or physical, he has been given, and this means, in effect, that he will be qualified for certain kinds of activity and not for others. It indicates for each his own vocational trend, and this, when one is striving to find one's centre, is already a valuable pointer.

The Buddhas have trodden the path beforehand. They have left a tradition as a compass to keep men facing in the right direction together with various 'means of grace' from the Noble Eightfold Program downward. What even the Buddhas do not do, however, is to travel in our place. Each must approach the centre in his own peculiar way, for the experience of each being is unrepeatable; every possibility in the universe is unique.

Let no one feel discouraged because his knowledge is as yet minute; rather let him think of enlarging it by every means in his power. Minute or not, it is a spark, and with a spark it is possible to kindle a still brighter lamp and thus pursue the way.

May that lamp grow, for each and all of us, till it has reached the brilliance and magnitude of a Vaisakh moon.[1]

NOTE

1 According to the Indian calendar, the full moon in the month of May, which marked the Buddha's enlightenment at the foot of the World Tree at Gaya

II

The Marriage of
Wisdom and Method

In order to illustrate the present theme I have drawn on two traditions, the Buddhist and the Christian; if such a juxtaposition of two very different pictures of the universe and of man's place in it implies something of a confrontation on the one hand, it also provides, on the other, a means of reciprocal confirmation across the bridge of contrast: all comparisons of orthodox, that is to say intrinsically valid, religious forms are able to serve this dual purpose.

Among the most salient differences between the two religions here in question are that, whereas in the Christian view the idea of Divine Personality dominates the scene together with its created counterpart, the human person, the Buddhist religious economy bypasses the former idea altogether while also picturing our human situation in a manner remote from the familiar ways of Western thinking; for it, that individual consciousness which we tend to equate with a constant personal entity appears as but an unstable aggregation of constituent factors involved in one overriding process of change, samsāra, the World's Flow: to know true personality, or true divinity for that matter (Buddhism would avoid both these terms), one must first awaken from one's existential dream; one who has done this is called *Buddha*, or the Awakened One. Meanwhile, to try and imagine what that supreme experience is like is only to entangle oneself further in the net of illusory conceptualism and the unending speculations it is for ever giving rise to.

A no less conspicuous difference can be seen in the respective attitudes of the two traditions to the question of sin, which with Christian thinkers through the ages has become an almost obsessive preoccupation. The classical definition of sin, to be found in any standard catechism, is the wilful disregard, by commission or omission, of a revealed law. 'Wilful' is the keyword here, for if an undesirable action arises out of sheer ignorance so that the will plays no part, then the word 'sin' will not apply, nor will such sanctions as would go with a given action if sinfully, that is to say wilfully, undertaken apply there either. Here obedience or else offence offered to the Divine Legislator, that God who is both justly merciful and mercifully just, will determine, for a Christian, his every moral valuation.

A Buddhist on the other hand, though by no means indifferent to sin (no religion could possibly minimise this vital issue), will assess all questions of offence, not by referring back to a divinely imparted law, but to the *nature of things*; no one judges our actions but ourselves or rather, to be more accurate, it is again the nature of things which will judge us because implacable judgement inheres in its very substance. Similarly, if there be a hell it is we who create it; having created it we should logically not be too surprised when we find ourselves trapped there until such time as the eschatological consequences of our misdeeds have played themselves out; similar considerations would of course apply to a paradise, as a recompense for righteous action. All this, for a Buddhist, forms part of the endless process of existential becoming; it is from the process itself, and not from certain of its symptoms, that he seeks deliverance and this, for him, can only come about through awareness of the true nature of the process itself or, as Buddhism prefers to put it, from a divestment of those persistent misconceptions which keep that process fuelled.

For one who views things thus, the to us familiar concept of forgiveness becomes practically unthinkable, being replaced by the idea of purification through knowledge; whereas for a Christian the divine prerogative to remit sins following on human repentance does evidently include the idea of purification as a consequence, for an adherent of the Buddhist religion it is knowledge alone which constitutes the lustral water wherewith to wash away the traces of sinful pollution in the human soul.

At this point in the argument one can, however, imagine someone chipping in with the question 'Does this nature of things to which you have alluded differ all that much from our own idea of "God", except by the absence of a personal attribution which, after all, may have remained latent simply because in the Buddhist wisdom there was no call to single it out?'

'Now you are asking something,' one would feel minded to reply, for indeed this question is a crucial one wherever inter-religious encounters are concerned and, moreover, this question contains the very means of reconciliation we all would fain discover in the present time of trouble, when for the first time in recorded history not just a certain religion but religion as such is under vicious attack. Better not attempt to elucidate this question further for the time being, but rather let it be allowed to act as a gentle ferment in one's mind so that the vintage of unforced under-standing may mature there in its own time. What has been said hitherto will, as one hopes, be enough by way of preparation for the more detailed discussion to follow.

To start off, let me recall an episode I heard mentioned at the time of the Dalai Lama's visit to Britain in the autumn of 1974. Someone had asked him how he felt about the Chinese invaders of Tibet; did he not hate them for the way they had treated and continued to treat his countrymen? The person putting this question doubtless expected some answer to the effect that the Buddha's teaching, like Christ's, excludes hatred and violence, even in return for a great wrong. But what he got was something quite different, of which the matter-of-factness must have astonished anyone used to the habitual emotionalism of Western moralists, for what the Lama said amounted to this: Do the Tibetans stand to benefit in some respect or other from hating the Chinese? Or alternatively, will the Chinese draw some benefit from being thus hated? And if neither party is to derive any advantage, what's the point, then, of hating?

This answer of the Dalai Lama, moreover, reflects an attitude that I and others have commonly observed among members of the Tibetan refugee community, most of whom, incidentally, are not ex-landlords and their like as alleged by propagandists out to whitewash the Chinese occupation but quite simple people belonging to peasant families – some are monks of course, most of whom also come from peasant stock, certainly not the kind of people to think up a sophisticated version of their own motivation.

One may well ask oneself whether such restraint in the face of brutal persecution could really be the outcome, not of some heroic exercise of human self-restraint, but of an apparently cold-blooded consideration of the data concerning the matter at issue. Could it be, as the Dalai Lama's remarks suggested, that an act of focused attention was enough in itself to charm away vindictive impulses which, for most people the world over, would seem almost excusable under the circumstances and in any case wellnigh irresistible?

Yet this is in fact the gist of the Dalai Lama's comment on that particular occasion, namely that the most potently intellectual and moral instrument to be found in man's psychological armoury is this very faculty of focused attention previously mentioned, the faculty of 'mindfulness', as it is usually called by Buddhists, without the cooperation of which, as they say, no other human virtue however sublime is able to be exercised with any sureness. For this reason mindfulness occupies a preeminent place in the Buddhist scale of values, so much so that most of the elementary techniques connected with meditation are concerned with fostering a habit of rhythmic attentiveness without trying to get this geared at the outset to anything like what we would call a spiritual theme. If some people are inclined to question the usefulness of such un-dramatic practices as watching the alternate inflow and outflow of one's breath for hours at a stretch, this is because the Christian injunction to pray, though not excluding in principle the possibility of such technical aids to attention, does not include as a matter of course, as happens in Buddhism, a technique for keeping sharp the tools to be used for this purpose; emphasis on the whole is laid on the objects of prayer, wisely coupled with encouragement to use canonic forms of prayer like the 'Our Father' and the 'Hail Mary', which undoubtedly have a power to regulate the human psyche far greater than any prayer improvised by the person himself; this should be said in passing.

The problem of distraction nevertheless will often arise and when this happens it is more than likely that the person so affected will be expected to rely immediately on the will, in the context of the Grace of God, in order to recall himself to a state of attention. Here Buddhists would be inclined to say that the human will, like anything else in one's psychic make-up, starts off already weakened by improper use and therefore requires intelligent training, failing which its action will remain too fluctuating to stand up to the pressures of distracting thoughts such as no man, be he English or Tibetan or other, can expect to be immune from. Ability to use the will effectively, which our moralists too readily take for granted, is not all that easy, it does not go without its corresponding skill which may in fact be equated with that very mindfulness we have just been discussing.

At this point one might even hazard an elementary definition of mindfulness by saying that it is the methodic application of intelligence to any and every human contingency from the most outward and everyday actions to those inward-looking operations that fall into the category of mystical experiences. It is therefore not unreasonable to posit the presence of mindfulness whenever there is question of exercising will-power rightly.

From the angle of mindfulness it should now be possible to consider some of the practical problems affecting a religiously intended life in this world, by taking our stand upon a principle which is basic to the teachings of the Great Way, Mahayana, this being the name collectively applied to the northern schools of Buddhism comprising the regions of China, Japan and Tibet, to which must be added Tibet's cultural offshoot in Mongolia, not forgetting the Kalmuks of the steppes west of the Caspian who form the only Buddhist group indigenous to Europe. The principle in question is expressed by saying that, for any human enterprise to be brought to good result, two mutually dependent factors have to be called into play to which are given the names of 'Wisdom' and 'Method'. This idea is further expressed by comparing Wisdom to the eye which discerns and Method to the legs which carry one along. There is a happy parable lending point to this moral, often quoted but which bears repetition; it runs as follows:

Two men set out to reach the city of Enlightenment but neither was able to make much progress because each was suffering from a serious disability; the one man was blind and the other man was lame. Eventually they hit on the idea of joining forces (one might have said of combining their disabilities), so the lame man climbed on the blind man's back after which they set out together, with the man who could see pointing out the way while the man with sound legs advanced along it, and thus they both arrived safely in the city.

Let us now turn to the consideration of the symbolism which has given its title to the present essay: 'the Marriage of Wisdom and Method'. This symbolism runs right through the sacred iconography of northern Buddhism and has been given the greatest extension in Tibetan art. What we are shown in countless frescoes on temple walls, in painted scrolls for domestic use, and in cast images are paired figures clasped in the ecstasy of union and holding certain objects in their hands, namely a bell and something like the thunderbolt of Jupiter as known to Graeco-Roman antiquity; this second object is called *vajrā* in Sanskrit, *dorje* in Tibetan, whence the name of Darjeeling, which means 'place of the *dorje*'. .

The bell is always associated with the female partner, who stands for Wisdom; the *dorje* with the male partner, representing Method. Within the general context of this symbolism, these erotic portraits represent variously named Buddhas with their celestial Consorts so that other details will vary to match their titles, but the Wisdom-cum-Method relationship is maintained overall.

When Christian missionaries first came in contact with these artistic creations their built-in prejudices led them to see in these paired figures some kind of pornographic motive, an abomination of the heathen; in fact images of this type are regarded by Tibetans as radiating a message of austerest purity – it is their critics who unwittingly revealed the baser instincts of their own prudish minds. However, apart from these anthropomorphic representations, Wisdom and Method are commonly symbolised by the two ritual objects already mentioned, both made of metal, namely the hand-bell and the *dorje*; every officiating monk or lama possesses these two objects, which are used both in temple worship and in all sorts of accessory rites; their detailed examination will help to throw their functional significance into sharper relief.

First the bell: this always bears the same devices and is cast in a special alloy yielding a clear and beautiful note ('the voice of wisdom'); as we have seen, the bell belongs to the female partner in the association. Its handle is crowned with the goddess-like head of Prajna Paramita, Wisdom Transcendent, here equated with Tara, the mother of Bodhisattvas or beings dedicated to Enlightenment who, in the Tibetan tradition, reproduces many of the characteristics which, in the Christian tradition, are associated with Mary – a case of spiritual coincidence, certainly not of historical borrowing. Self-evidently, every man born of woman is a potential

Bodhisattva; it but remains for him to turn this potentiality of his into an actuality by ripening his wisdom through a deploying of the appropriate method. The latter will necessarily vary somewhat from person to person, since no two beings are alike nor can their path to the Centre be quite identical; this also should be noted. The voice of the bell is an invitation to us all to undergo transformation into a truly human being, failing which one remains human in principle, but subhuman in fact.

As for the *dorje*: this consists of a central shaft flanked by four (sometimes subdivided into eight) flanges, with a constriction where the right hand grasps it in the middle. These lateral flanges correspond to the four directions of space which between them 'encompass' the universe. Here we evidently have to do with an *axial* symbol, of which the implications are far-reaching. In fact, a precisely similar symbolism belongs to the three-dimensional Cross, whereof the *dorje* is but a variant. Christians should always remember this metaphysical meaning attaching to the central emblem of their tradition, for the Cross, by thus 'measuring' the worlds, already proclaims the truth that one who is raised upon the Cross shall be both Judge – to measure something implies sitting in judgement – and Saviour.

The salvational message of the Cross springs out of its very structure: first we have the upright, corresponding to the universal axis as such, which must be conceived as extending indefinitely in both directions and thus connecting together all possible levels of existence, all worlds, all beings. Read from above downward the axis traces the path of Grace, the attractive influence of Heaven as the Chinese sages have it; read from below upwards it indicates the homeward path to be followed by those who, having been touched by Grace, wish to retrace it to its source. All that we call 'spiritual life' is summed up in this two-way traffic between Heaven and Earth: such is the message of the Cross's upright.

Second, we have the transverse beam of the Cross, representing for its part a particular degree of individual existence and notably the human degree as such; to complete the scheme one would have to imagine an indefinite series of such transverse branchings corresponding to other existential degrees in all their variety, but, symbolically speaking, the one transverse example suffices to illustrate the essential relationship to the axis, which will hold good for all other comparable cases.

As with the Cross, the same symbolical features are recognisable in the form of the *dorje*, with the handgrip corresponding to the Cross's intersection and carrying the selfsame human implications. Given man's situation at this point on the Cross's central shaft, it can be seen that his intrinsic vocation is to serve as a connecting-link between Earth and Heaven and, in virtue of this unique prerogative, to act as an advocate with the higher Powers for all his fellow beings dwelling at lower, that is to say more limiting, existential levels; to regard himself as being merely their exploiter is a flagrant betrayal of his own status. The frequent reference, in the Buddhist sacred writings, to 'human birth hard to obtain' reflects this situation; to be so privileged and yet fritter away this precious opportunity in trivial pursuits makes no sense; one may well ask oneself, 'Why then does this happen to us so often?' A man must be worse than complacent to suppose that he can neglect such an opportunity and yet stay where he is in the scale of existence; a fall from such a height is bound to take one to a depth proportionately abysmal; it seems no more than logical to say so.

I remember once hearing a lama say that with the first inkling of one's own ignorance one is already one step forward in the path of knowledge: this has doubtless been said before, but it cannot be repeated too often. Once such an awareness dawns upon one's mind one is immediately faced with a choice: shall I continue as before or shall I turn in my tracks (which is what the word 'conversion' means literally)? Here the will can have an important part to play, for if this first impulse to reconsider one's life be a grace (as it must be, seeing that it was no initiative of one's own that evoked it), it is still not an automatic certainty that one will respond to that grace positively; where there is a choice the will, informed by intelligence or else confused by ignorance, will necessarily enter in. However, assuming that one decides to heed the mysterious call, the next step is bound to take the form of asking oneself the question 'What must I do now? How can I find out?' This amounts to a request for method: wherever there is a 'what?' or a 'how?' method must needs take a hand. Nevertheless, the earliest step of all is always a manifestation of wisdom, corresponding to a grace; and so will be the end of the road, after method has given all it had to give, when Wisdom Transcendent will shine of its own light.

The important thing to note here is that the first step in the direction of man's true home will typically be a negative one; one turns away from something in favour of something else, one abjures a life governed by profane preoccupations in order to seek the knowledge which comes when the human ego has ceased to treat itself as divine in its own right. In order to fit oneself for the exacting task ahead one finds oneself compelled to undergo some sort of discipline not of one's own devising, a scheme of do's and don'ts, and this is precisely what the outward prescriptions of a religion do for one, their purpose being to steady the being throughout his or her earthly sojourn. It is nevertheless possible to see further into these same prescriptions, by tapping their latently symbolic potential; treated intelligently, a religious law need not seem irksome; but in any case its rough and its smooth should be accepted as part of an organic traditional whole.

We live in an age when there has been a wholesale repudiation of whatever belongs to the formal order, be it linked to the practice of a religion or ostensibly social in its bearing. Where people have not cast away their ancestors' religious allegiance altogether in order to align themselves with those who regard the idea of a spiritual order as totally outmoded, they have been attracted in increasing numbers to cults offering mystical experiences on the cheap, that is to say minus any requirement that the would-be disciple should adhere to that religious form where the esoteric teachings he seeks originated and from the traditional armoury of which his instructors in these teachings will draw all their instruments; for the disciple, moreover, his adherence to the appropriate religious form will constitute his guarantee that what he is being offered is genuine: beware of a professing 'master' who offers a Sufism without Islam or a Tibetan Tantric initiation without Buddhism, or the Jesus Prayer without Christianity for that matter.

But the converse also applies: it would be equally improper for a Christian to ask for a Buddhist *mantram* or for a Buddhist to start invoking the Divine Name in Arabic like the members of a Sufi confraternity. One can deeply revere the same truth when uttered in a foreign language but this does not mean that one can pick and choose from several languages at random; to respect the internal purity of each is also a way of showing reverence. As for oneself, surely one religious language correctly spoken is enough.

This present paper was completed late one evening: next morning I attempted to sum up its conclusions in a few parting words.

For any man, his state of wisdom will coincide with his ability to direct an unflickering mindfulness upon whatever happens to come his way – in Christian terms, with his ability to see God everywhere and at all times and to shape both judgements and behaviour accordingly. 'Faith' is that intermediate mode of knowledge which, at any given stage of life, fills for us the gap between mere belief and that unlimited awareness known to Buddhists as 'Enlightenment'. It has been said of faith that, besides light, it comprises an aspect of obscurity; it can readily be understood why this must be so, pending the moment when one will 'see not in a glass darkly, but face to face', as St Paul puts it. *Method* covers all that will be conducive to a state of wisdom at any degree: pre-eminently Method provides us with the opportunity to *verify* those truths we hold by faith through expressing them onto-logically, that is to say in terms of our own being.

Conformably with the traditional symbolism, Enlightenment coincides with the consummation of the marriage of Wisdom and Method; if this statement sounds rather final, it does nevertheless leave room for an awareness towards which what has been said hitherto has all along been converging, namely recognition of the truth that, as between the twin principles that have provided the subject of our present discussion, there exists no actual barrier of otherness; this distinction, though valid and therefore useful on its own showing, can be transcended in the knowledge that Method, statically conceived, is none other than Wisdom; Wisdom, dynamically conceived, may properly be called Method. For a man of ripened intelligence, Method *is* Wisdom, Wisdom *is* Method: readers familiar with the Heart Sutra will surely recognise the parallel implications. Such an awareness, once awakened, can never be put to sleep again, though a sinful unmindfulness may overlay it, in which case it continues to work like an abscess that has become tightly enclosed, until a true *metanoia* allows it to come out again into the open. When left unimpeded, this same truth can transfigure a man, colouring his perceptions as fast as they arise and con-ditioning his every activity. Even when only incipient, a knowledge of the ultimate identity of Wisdom and Method is already a power-ful means of gaining freedom from that obsessive compartmenting of attention between the notional and the bodily side of things, abstract thought and involvement in action, which has been responsible for so much damage in this world of ours. By living out this truth both as contemplation, when one can fairly call it 'Wisdom', and practically, as Method, one can be brought to the threshold of that Mystery of which the Buddha has unlocked the door. Nothing that we can do or say or think escapes from this twofold need; the whole teaching about Wisdom and Method turns on satisfying that need, daily and hourly.

III

Is There a Problem
of Evil?

When we pose the question 'Is there a problem of evil?' we are
not doing so with the intention of charming away evil with words,
still less of relieving our minds of the sense of sin, as modern
psychology is more and more tending to do; nor are we concerned
with a merely comforting mental adjustment nor with what
people refer to as 'happiness', to which moreover they suppose
themselves to have a 'right'.

On the contrary, for us, evil corresponds to a reality at the level
of the world, and so does 'sin', in the religious sense of a voluntary
disregard of a revealed law. Likewise 'goodness', in the ordinary
sense, though often vaguely conceived and expressed, corresponds
to a reality at this level. In fact, the two things belong together, as
members of a duality, as shadow belongs to light and cannot
help doing so. All this may be taken for granted in the present
instance.

However, what we are now concerned with is whether or not
evil constitutes a 'problem', one that supposedly is still awaiting a
satisfactory solution. It cannot be denied that this opinion has often
been put forward, consciously or, still more often, unconsciously
– the phrase 'problem of evil' is one of the commonest clichés in the
language – and furthermore religious writers, especially in the
Christian Church, have frequently felt constrained to offer more or
less satisfying solutions to this supposed problem, of which a
typical example is the statement, theologically valid but vulnerable
to sentimental stultification, that God 'permits' evil in view of a
greater good. 'Why does the world not contain only good, only

joy?' is a question constantly cropping up through the ages. 'Why was it not created free from evil, pain and anxiety?'

When shorn of all accessory considerations, the alleged problem reduces itself to the following dilemma: God is said to be almighty and all good; He is also called the creator of the world. If He is good but yet created a world as evil and unhappy as the one we see around us, then He cannot be almighty; if on the other hand He is almighty and still created the world thus, then He cannot be all good.

In their time, the Manicheans and kindred sects known to early Christian history, on the basis of such reasoning, concluded that the demiurge, the world's creator, must be an intrinsically evil being, certainly not God Himself. Trying thus to shift the blame, they still left the essential problem unsolved, since they did not tell us how or why the demiurgic tendency itself either arose in the first instance, in the face of God, or was able to operate. In fact these sects were obsessed with this particular problem, and their attempts to find an answer satisfying to human feeling often led them into strangely contradictory enunciations. It is not with these desultory attempts, condemned by the Church, that we are concerned today, for in the religious crisis through which the world is now passing the basic dilemma takes a different and more far-reaching form; in fact, behind it lurks the thought, as an implicit conclusion, that if things are so then God is neither almighty nor good nor creator, for He does not exist. The world is a blind place then, a field of blind forces whose playthings we, and all our fellow beings, are and must needs remain. If during past ages, when faith was relatively general, people hesitated to draw the conclusion in this naked form and therefore resorted to various intellectual subterfuges in order to avoid it, that conclusion was there all the same potentially, a seed waiting to germinate whenever it found itself in a soil conditioned to receive it; the unuttered thought was like a perpetual chink in the armour of belief, and the various dialectical expedients resorted to during times when the human mind was still predisposed to accept the theological premises were never quite sufficient to plug this gap in man's spiritual defences. One is speaking, of course, chiefly of the Christian world; in the Indian traditions the problem, if indeed it existed at all, never assumed this acute form for reasons to be explained later but, as we are living in an environment formed on the basis of Christian concepts and still predominantly governed by Christian values, it is necessary, and indeed inevitable, for us to concern ourselves with the consequences of Christian thought, or lack of thought, on this vital subject. We are living through an age of doubt, if not of 'counter-faith', and this makes it more than ever imperative for us to think clearly, if we are able, concerning a question with which the spreading attitude of doubt is causally bound up, at least in large measure. Before we can think of discovering an answer, however, we must first make sure the question itself has been properly put; for unless such is in fact the case, it would be idle to expect a proper solution.

Indeed, many of the unresolved problems that plague men's minds, and especially those of a metaphysical order – the ultimate questions concerning selfhood and existence – are not merely unsolved but insoluble because they have in fact been faultily set. There is a catch in the statement of the problem itself, and this precludes the possibility of an answer. A question badly put – to quote one eminent commentator of our time, Frithjof Schuon – does not call forth light any more than it derives from light. Half the urgent questions that keep tormenting us would evoke their own answer spontaneously, if only they could once be correctly framed.

Such is the question now before us. What we are presently attempting to do is in fact to improve the framing of this question of evil, as an indispensable prelude to any eventual answering of it.

Before proceeding with our discussion, however, there is one further remark to offer; the evidence that will be laid before the reader, doctrinal, illustrative, or dialectical, is drawn from many different sources. Little is attributable to myself personally, except the manner of presenting it. In any case, the truth belongs to all equally, in proportion to each man's power – and willingness – to assimilate it (this was said by René Guénon); there is no room for claims of human originality in respect of the truth itself, except in this sense, namely that whoever succeeds in expounding any aspect of truth is original in virtue of that very fact, and necessarily so. It is also good to remember that the effective realisation of truth in any circumstances will always entail more than an operation of mere thought. Such a realisation, as saints and sages are forever reminding us, will always imply an equating of being and knowing; it must never be supposed that the thinking faculty amounts to the total intelligence of a being, though it is a mode of intelligence in an indirect sense and useful in its own sphere, which is that field of relativities whereof the manifested world consists. True intelligence, which alone deserves the name of intellect unqualified, is a faculty which, if it be not hindered as a result of insubordination by the lesser faculties, its appointed handmaids, will fly straight to the mark. It does not 'think'; it sees. The catalysing of this power to see, which everyone bears within himself whether he be aware of it or not, is the aim of all spiritual method, its only aim. Correct framing of a necessary question, so that the evidence supplies itself and hence also the answer or proof, can act as such a catalytic agent. That is why a discussion like the present one can on occasion be fruitful; otherwise it were better to keep silent. Of purposeless discussion the world has more than enough.

But let us now go back to the dilemma concerning the Creator's power and His goodness, as propounded above. We said that behind it lay concealed the thought that this apparent contradiction was tantamount to a dethroning of God, to be replaced, as the ultimate and only principle in the universe, by a blind becoming, a view from which a determinism governed by chance alone would moreover seem to follow inescapably.

It is, then, a rather startling fact that at the very time when theories of this kind seemed to be gaining ground in the world of science and among the educated classes generally – I will not call them intellectual – and in a more diffuse and instinctive form among the urban masses, another type of theory should have gained credence whereby something like an optimistic bias is attributed to the course of the universe and to the shaping of its contents, a bias working in a (to us) pleasing direction, by a passage from simple to complex (complex being equated with superior) and culminating, up to date, in mankind as we know it, though, of course, with the implication that further developments in the same sense are to be expected in an indefinite future. I am referring to the body of theories that come under the heading of evolutionism, of which the Darwinian theory was but one specification among others, one that created the stir it did largely because of its timing, having supplied just the kind of explanation people were looking for at that moment, especially in the sociological sphere where the doctrines in question are associated with the name of 'progress'. It provided, as it were, a scientific sanction, supported by much tangible evidence, to an already existing wish, and this conjunction carried it far on the road to general acceptance within a very short time.

Evolution, whatever truths or fallacies the word may enshrine, has become, to all intents and purposes, a dogma of the modern age – in some countries its open denial might even land a man in jail – and though scientists themselves may discuss its premises in this or that context, the public at large takes it as much for granted, as a glance at the daily press shows, as any medieval public took for granted certain dogmas of the Church, even while oversimplifying their meaning. As Gai Eaton wrote: 'The ages of faith are always with us, only their object changes.' Here the word 'faith', of course, must be understood loosely as meaning belief, since faith in its deeper (and more accurate) sense is far more than that, indicating that indirect and participative knowledge that must fill the gap between knowing and being, theoretical assent and realisation, so long as the two exist apart; once they are unified, by the miracle of intellection, there is no more seeing in a glass darkly, but only face to face, in the noonday of truth.

Now, this mention of the evolutionary doctrines has a purpose that ties up with the subject of this essay. I am not concerned to discuss the applicability of these doctrines as such. What I wish to illustrate, by this passing reference, is that they imply, under all their differing forms, acceptance of a kind of universal trend toward the better, which here is represented as an inherent property of becoming, the good itself being always an ideal perceived some distance ahead but presumably never actually attainable, since this would terminate the evolutionary process in a seemingly arbitrary manner. It is noteworthy that with every fresh discovery of science, every invention and especially those that present a sensational aspect as with rockets to the moon, etc., this idea of the upward evolution of humanity is evoked as a kind of mystique, and the same occurs in respect of the more important social developments. If it be objected that some of these happenings are by no means so certainly beneficial as their sponsors would have it, that is not the point, since what we are trying to observe is a certain trend in the general mentality, very marked in our time, which, because of its reading of an optimistic bias into the unfolding of the universe, runs flatly counter to the other logical implications of a materialist determinism, of a universe conceived as functioning minus God. That two such opposed assumptions should be able to coexist in a selfsame mind, as they so often do, is a highly significant piece of evidence, since it shows, for one thing, that the 'problem' of good and evil, or superior and inferior if one so prefers, is still very much with us and as far from a solution as ever.

There is really no logical reason for believing in a survival value attaching to what is good, rather than to what is evil (one cannot avoid using these terms here, imprecise as they are); nor is there any evident basis for the supposition that a blind universe, one that reflects no principle superior to its becoming, somehow carries within itself a preference in favour of what we men regard as 'good' – on the basis of our own feelings. Indeed, there is a very considerable weight of evidence against such an opinion, at least sufficient to preclude any facile assumption in its favour. Hence it is reasonable to conclude that behind the belief in question there lies some kind of sentimental motive, such as has influenced both the selecting and the reading of the evidence in a manner that cannot be described as purely scientific – to be 'scientific' implies above all impartiality – and this again goes to show that man is still tormented with the pressing problem of his present unhappiness, for which he tries to compensate by projecting onto the future his own yearning for a universe organised so that he will not suffer; in other words, a 'good' world or a happy world.

The picture that this calls up, if one pauses to think, is so reminiscent of the carrot swinging in view of the donkey to make it pull the cart ever farther that one cannot help asking oneself who, in that case, is the driver of the cart, the one who placed the carrot where it is? This also is in its way a pertinent question.

The stage has now been sufficiently set to allow us to come to grips with our initial question: 'Is there a problem of evil?' as the saying still goes. It is best to leave aside individual speculations and turn, for light, to the teachings of the great traditions and see what they have to offer by way of an answer. In treating their sacred narratives and other symbolical expressions, however, we must be ready from the start to look beyond the letter, to read between the lines, to find, side by side with the more literal interpretation (valid at its own level), that deep-searching interpretation that Dante called 'anagogical' as pointing the way to the heights of mystical realisation. (The word 'mystical' here must be given its root meaning of 'silent', of a knowledge inexpressible because escaping the limits of form). To this knowledge the sacred forms – forms, that is to say, drawing their spiritual efficacy from the fact that they are founded upon true analogies between different orders of reality – serve as provisional pointers. Their providential usefulness is to provide keys to the mysteries; as such, they are not to be decried, as so often happens, in the name of some mental abstraction or other that would have itself 'pure spirit', but rather they must be treated as the good craftsman treats the tools of his trade, by guarding them against such impairment as a strait-laced literalism, on the one side, or profane denigration, on the other, may have wished upon them. This all has a close bearing on the currently imputed failure of religion and the consequent neglect, by disheartened men, of means provided for the sake of the only task that matches the human condition – means that have to be formal by the very fact that we ourselves are beings endowed with form.

In order to illustrate our chosen theme, it is fitting, with an audience largely composed of Christians or of people moulded more or less by Christian thought, that we should turn first of all to the evidence contained in the earliest chapters of the Book of Genesis, those that give the story of Adam and Eve. No more illuminating symbolical narrative is to be found in all sacred literature.

Here we see the Tree of Life, corresponding to the axis of the universe, standing in the midst of the garden in which Adam, primordial man, dwells at peace with all his fellow beings, the animals and plants of the garden. Through him they participate in the centre, represented by the tree; so long as his attention remains focused there, there is no disharmony or fear anywhere, and as far as anyone can tell this state of affairs will continue indefinitely. Here we see the image of *perfect participation in passive mode*. (Of participation in active mode we shall have something to say later.)

But now there comes along the serpent, offering to Adam a hitherto untasted experience, that of fragmented unity, of things unreferred to the centre and valued for their own sake as if they were self-sufficing entities. This was, and still remains, the characteristic lure of the Tree of Knowledge of Good and Evil. Adam, persuaded by Eve at the instance of the serpent, tastes of the fruit, and behold in a moment his pristine purity of intent is lost, and he and Eve suddenly become conscious of all that divides them from themselves and from one another and consequently also from each and every thing around them. From that moment on they both feel imprisoned within their own fragmentary consciousness, their empirical ego, and this fact is evidenced by their shame at their own nakedness, which they try to cover up with an artificial selfhood of their own contriving, the fig leaves that have become the prototype of all human disguise.

And as for the Tree of Life, what has become of it? For it no longer is, as far as Adam and Eve are concerned. Looking where they expect to behold it, they can discern only that other tree, the Tree of Good and Evil bowing under the weight of its fruits light and dark, containing the seeds of indefinite becoming. Advisedly we said 'that other tree', since for the first time they feel an acute sense of otherness, of *I* and *you*, and by this very fact they are cut off from those other beings with whom they formerly had communed on free and fearless terms.

What they fail to perceive, however, is the real identity of the tree itself; this is a vital point in this highly symbolic story. Indeed, I myself remember as a child at school feeling much puzzled by this unexplained appearance in the garden of a second tree; it was not till years after I was grown up that it dawned on me that there never had been a second tree but that it was the same tree seen double, through the distorting glass of ignorance. Regarded from the viewpoint of ignorance, the Tree of Life *becomes* the Tree of Knowledge of Good and Evil; regarded from the viewpoint of true knowledge, the Tree of Becoming (as it might just as well be called) *is* the Tree of Life.

Here we have a complete metaphysical doctrine, in its essentials, expressed through the biblical narrative. And how effective to communicate is this concrete symbolism of a tree, or trees, in comparison with the abstractions dear to the philosophic mind!

But now we have been led back to our initial dilemma. Apologists who have wished to defend God (!) against an accusation of being 'the author of evil' – and many have felt constrained so to defend Him – have missed one vital point: the paradise, happy as it was, *contained the serpent*. Nothing is said in the narrative itself to account for this startling fact, which occurs almost casually at the moment when the fatal event is about to take place.

Yet if one pauses to look really closely into the premises of creation, one must surely wake up to the truth that a paradise –

any paradise – to be a paradise *must contain the serpent*. I admit I did not discover this for myself; it was pointed out to me. The perfection of a paradise without the presence of the serpent would be the perfection, not of paradise, but of God Himself. It would be, in Sufic terms, 'the paradise of the Essence'. Therefore when one says of a paradise (or anything else) that it is created good or perfect, this can only mean that it is good or perfect *as far as a paradise* (or other created thing) *is able to be perfect*.

Moreover, the same principle will apply in the case of a hell. A hell, to be a hell, must contain a trace of the Tree of Life concealed in it somewhere; it cannot be a place of absolute evil or absolute imperfection or absolute anything. That is why, in the Tibetan iconography for instance, when hells are depicted, a Buddha is always also shown there, as a necessary, if latent, witness to the omnipresent truth.

The essential principle to grasp is that wherever one is dealing with a *relative* perfection, one that has existential limits, one has implicitly accepted a degree of imperfection in respect of the absence of whatever lies outside those limits. This privative character of the limit is manifested, within any limit, by a proneness to change and consequent suffering. This is a basic thesis of Buddhism, but it is not less a thesis, if differently expressed, of the Semitic traditions. Let it be remembered that even Christ on occasion said, 'Why callest thou me good?' What he was in fact affirming by these words was the genuineness of his own human state, in the presence of his essential divinity. When it is said of Christ that he is 'true God, true Man', this necessarily implies, in respect of the second term, an existential limitation, therefore also a certain aspect of imperfection inseparable from the relative as such. Were this limit not there, as expressed in the fact that the Son of Man, Jesus, was able to become and to suffer, the humanity of Christ would have remained a mere phantom – there have been sects holding this view – and his incarnation would have been meaningless. In the human person of Christ we see therefore the perfect figure of humanity including its limitations. By definition the suchness of man is not the suchness of God; hence it cannot be called 'good' in its own right but only inasmuch as it reveals the divine perfection, first by existing at all and secondly by its symbolism.

In purely metaphysical terms this truth of Christianity can be expressed most succinctly by saying that in Christ absolute perfection and relative perfection meet. The intersection of the cross is the symbol of their perfect coincidence.

From all this it can be seen that our original question 'Is there a problem of evil?' by dint of closer scrutiny has undergone a shift of emphasis, since enough has been said to show that what manifests itself as 'evil' relatively to our human situation has its roots, cosmically speaking, further back in an imperfection inseparable from all manifestation as such, be it in the shape of a world, an individual being, or even a paradise. When the Sufis declare that 'paradise is a prison for the Sage just as the world is a prison for the believer', they are voicing their ultimate dissatisfaction with all that is not God while at the same time claiming to be something of its own.

It would then appear as if the question to be put should rather take the form of asking, 'Why does God create at all? Why is there any manifestation, any world? In fact, why need we exist?'

Now, before deciding whether such a question is a proper one or not, it is important to stress the fact that whenever divine action is spoken of, that action must be regarded as *necessary* as well as *free*; *in divinis* the two attributes coincide at every point whereas, with us, existence, which relativises everything, renders them more or less incompatible in any given set of circumstances. God's infinity implies absolute liberty; where there is no limit, there can be no constraint either. Likewise God's absoluteness implies limitless necessity; it is absurd to speak as if God's ordinances bore an arbitrary character, though the anthropomorphic symbolism sometimes may seem to suggest such an interpretation, a matter of expression only, which ought not to deceive any reasonable mind.

If then the creative act has been described, theologically, as 'gratuitous', this is intended to affirm God's absolute freedom and certainly not to deny His infinite necessity. The best one can say, therefore, about manifestation is that the infinite nature of the divine possibility evidently includes it and therefore also requires it; were it not so, the infinite would not be itself. This must, however, never be taken as meaning that the world, by existing, has added something to God or that its eventual disappearance will indicate a proportional privation concerning the Divine, for the relative in itself amounts to nothing in the presence of the real, though by its own limited reality it manifests the real at a given level, failing which it would not exist. As for the question why do things exist, it is devoid of intrinsic sense; our existence is not something to which the question 'Why?' can validly be attached in expectation of a solution comfortable to human logic, itself an apanage of the existence in question. Existence is something one can accept only for what it is. All argument about things starts from there; it cannot be pushed further back thanks to some more than usually ingenious subterfuge of the discursive mind. Only the eye of intellect – the 'third eye' of Indian traditional symbolism – is able to pierce beyond the existential veil because something of what lies beyond is already to be found in its own substance; it is not for nothing that Meister Eckhardt called it 'uncreate and uncreatable'. But here we are outside the discursive realm altogether.

The only comment to be offered – and it constitutes a perfectly adequate answer to a question in itself senseless – is that, as long as existence (or creation) is a possibility (as it evidently is at its own level), that possibility will in due course be called to manifestation for the reason we have already given, namely that the divine all-possibility cannot be limited in any manner whatsoever. This is enough to account for the existence of the relative, the cosmic unfolding in all its indefinitude of becoming, including that apparent opposing of relative to real, of world to God, that constitutes, for beings, their separative dream. Better reply we cannot find, but this one surely is good enough.

It now remains for us to consider in turn, though very briefly, what the chief traditions have to say on the subject of evil, since each will inevitably look at it from its own angle, offering comment attuned to its own spiritual dialect and technique. The unanimous testimony is to be found at the centre, where all ways meet.

So far, we have chiefly drawn examples from the Christian tradition for obvious reasons, with passing references to the sister traditions. Here, all that needs to be added on the subject of Christianity is that the idea of 'a problem' of evil originated there and is largely confined to that field. This idea is closely bound up with the anthropomorphic representation of the relationship between human and Divine, which, if pushed too far or insufficiently corrected by commentaries of a more purely sapiential kind (as in the sermons of Meister Eckhardt, for instance), can easily become invaded by sentimental and moralistic influences. To say this is in no wise to blame the anthropomorphic symbolism as such, which has not only proved its usefulness in the course of ages but also offers certain undoubted advantages for many souls. If it has its dangers, this is true of every form of expression, however hallowed; the serpent will be there, in some form or other.

There is only one defence against the kind of doctrinal abuses we are thinking of, those which in the Christian world, especially in modern times, have troubled and even alienated many minds, and this is by a return to the central themes of the doctrine, to its metaphysical heartland. Sentimental and rationalistic confusions invariably arise in the periphery of a tradition; it is an excessive preoccupation with marginal matters that tends to provoke them. Too many rather trivial considerations habitually occupy Christian minds to the neglect of the essential. Christian theology has been relegated dangerously to the status of a 'speciality', a matter for professionals and experts, instead of being regarded as the daily food for every soul which it really is. In this respect the Eastern traditions, despite the degeneration of the times which has not spared them, have much to teach regarding the day-to-day practice of religion. At Kalimpong, in the northern hills of Bengal where I lived for three years, my gardener (who was no saint) possessed a metaphysical and theological sense that many a bishop might have shared with advantage. The things he saw around him were far more transparent to his intelligence than is usually the case among religious people here. In that sense he could see God everywhere; theology was, for him, both a living and a practical pursuit. His devotion, such as it was, had an undoubted intellectual quality.

Only too often Christian devotion has been kept starved of intellectual nourishment, with the result that it has readily slipped into sentimentalism, and this in its turn has tended to drive out of the Christian fold many of the more intelligent minds, with disastrous results for themselves and for the world; but the fact is that, though these people may have been, in one sense, too intelligent to accept the heavily sweetened food that their religious mentors thought they wanted, yet in another sense they were not quite intelligent enough to detect, through the sugar, the salt that was still there waiting to be tasted.

One can only repeat it: a Christian revival without a renewal of intellectual penetration of the central truths is a chimera. Collective sentimentality will not bring it about, if indeed it does not hinder it further. It is time the leaders of the church recognised this; otherwise they will remain blind leading the blind, despite their sincere wish to serve. There is no substitute for knowledge.

To return to the Christian attitude toward evil: exoterically and in conformity with the anthropomorphic symbolism, Christian teaching has largely been content to say that God 'is not the author of evil', which, for its part, came about thus and thus. This view, though it contains flaws, is nevertheless justified, inasmuch as God does not will evil qua evil, evil as it appears to us. He is the creator of the relative, as required by His infinity; of that relative the thing we call evil is a necessary function, being in fact the measure of the world's apparent separation from its principle, God – an illusory separation inasmuch as nothing can exist side by side with the infinite, however real it may claim to be at its own relative level. To quote Frithjof Schuon, who has thrown the greatest light upon this question – his books are treasuries of spiritual discernment – 'One cannot ask of God to will the world and at the same time to will that it be not a world.' A world is a whirlpool of contrasts (the Indian word *samsāra* expresses this), it is not a unity in its own right. It is no limitation on the Almighty that He cannot produce another Himself, a second Absolute. The world is there to prove it.

Passing now to another Semitic tradition, Islam, we will find that it follows a somewhat different line. The central testimony of Islam is the unity and absolute transcendence of God, a truth that it shares with Christianity but stresses, if anything, in a more exclusive way than in any other tradition; hence it is obliged to declare, without turning aside, that whatever exists in any sense whatsoever is unequivocally the creation of God and therefore that evil, since it exists, is to be numbered among God's creatures.

If Christian theology on the whole shrank from such a plain statement and wished to wrap it up for the reasons we know of, Islam did not avoid it for another good reason – both reasons are valid but relative, hence their mutual exclusion. Indeed, where relativities are concerned, such divergencies are unavoidable and moreover necessary, since truth is one and discernment is a function of intelligence as such, in the light of truth. In this way, differentiation of witness, as between the various traditions, serves to reveal the converging nature of the various spiritual paths and their meeting at the centre, in the heart of truth.

The existence of the relative has this positive merit, offsetting its limiting or negative function, namely that it precludes our taking ourselves or the world for absolute, in other words, for God. The same applies in the field of doctrine. To attribute an absolute character to a form or other relativity is of the very nature of error, by fixing or 'petrifying' a limit and its attendant oppositions. Hence the teaching of Islam that 'the variety of the interpreters is also a blessing'. This statement contains no condemnation of orthodoxy, or of forms as necessary and legitimate instruments, but it bears witness to that variety in testimony that is one of the factors guaranteeing the unity of revelation.

The Muslims have also said: 'When the gates of Paradise were opened the 'gates of Hell were opened at the same time.' How often do we hear a wish expressed that God had made heaven but no hell; how many people expressing their belief in heaven couple this with a refusal to entertain any belief in hell. Here again is a case of failing to recognise that two things belong together, as correlatives pertaining to the same order. To deny this is implicitly to deny the Absolute, by wishing to endow one particular relativity with an absolute character while refusing relative existence to its normal partner; it is but another form of the error that would have God create a paradise minus the serpent.

All relativity can, and indeed must, ultimately be transcended, not by arbitrary denial but by integration. The world cannot just be charmed away, but it can be rendered transparent so that the light, ever shining, may illuminate our existential darkness. The centre is everywhere, this room included; and, where the centre is, there is the beatific vision.

Passing now to the Indian traditions, it will be found that the viewpoint differs considerably, inasmuch as the general concept of manifestation is not linked to the more particular concept of 'creation', as in the Semitic religions. The Hindus, when they attribute creative activity to the Divinity under one or other of its aspects, liken this to a 'divine playing', which is a way of affirming the unqualified freedom and transcendence of the Godhead in its unmanifest and impersonal essence, versus those dynamic, creative, and therefore qualifiable aspects of Divinity that correspond to the personal God of western spiritual parlance.

In Buddhism, where the idea of creation is practically absent, the personal aspect is as if 'bypassed' in the case of both the divine prototype and the human being. The 'nontheistic' (not atheistic) character of the Buddhist wisdom and its insistence on the 'non-selfhood' of all things belong together, a fact that moreover explains Buddhism's marked preference for apophatic enunciations. Dogmatic affirmations, by lending to ideas a kind of fixed self, are, from a Buddhist point of view, always suspect, if not in practice avoidable altogether. The Hindu tradition, on the other hand, with the maternal exuberance that characterises it, is able to accommodate all manner of doctrines such as, in other traditions, would tend to exclude one another; thus, for example, the Vedanta stands near to Buddhism in the rigorously impersonal nature of its appeal, while Vishnuite Hinduism and the bhaktic doctrines generally come much nearer to a personal religion in the Western sense. In practice Hinduism is able to associate both the personal and the impersonal approach in a synthesis that allows of an almost endless variety of combinations.

The manifested world, or worlds, as viewed through Indian eyes, does not, as we have said, require in principle to be given the character of a willed making or 'creation'. In Buddhism, where this idea (as already pointed out) practically finds no place, *samsāra*, the Round of Existence, is described as having 'no beginning' but as 'having an end'; in other words, the process of continual passage from cause to effect is left undefined in terms of origin, but that process and its associated possibility of suffering can be neutralised by integration into the centre 'where the wheel of rebirth is not turning'. Negatively regarded, this will be nirvanic extinction or self-naughting; positively regarded, it is the awakening to enlightenment, Buddhahood. Compare with this the Christian view representing the other extreme, namely the description of the world as having 'a beginning' (in creation) but as able to become 'world without end', in salvation through Christ. One metaphysical paradox is worth another, since, strictly speaking, beginning and ending belong to the same duality; their dissociation in either direction is metaphysically inconceivable. The paradoxical character of both the above-mentioned enunciations is explainable in terms of a spiritual purpose, a call to realisation; neither of them should be driven too far in literalism, but each expresses truth in its own way.

The mentality fostered by both Hinduism and Buddhism is not such as to see a problem in evil or suffering, as has happened elsewhere, because a sense of the relative and its ambivalent character, at once a veil over the absolute and a revealer thereof, of a reality at one level and an illusion at another, is too strongly ingrained in Indian thought to allow of evil being regarded as anything more than a particular case of the relative, viewed from its privative angle. Suffering in all its forms is then accepted as a measure of the world's apparent remoteness from the divine principle. The principle is absolutely omnipresent in the world, but the world is relatively absent from the principle, this apparent contradiction between 'essence' and 'accidents' is paid for in 'suffering'. By identifying ourselves, consciously or unconsciously or by our actions, with our 'accidents', whereby a specious selfhood is both created and nourished, we invite an inescapable repercussion in the form of the good and evil that consequently shape our lives for us while we are swept along by the stream of becoming. So long as that stream continues to flow, in the passage from action to con-cordant reaction, suffering will be experienced in positive or negative form, as unwanted presence of the painful or else as absence of the desirable. The nature of *samsāra*, the world's flow, is such, and no effort or contrivance on our part can render it otherwise. One can shift given evils to one side (life in this world often compels one to do so), or one can promote certain good objects – often at the price of neglecting others – but the process itself we never touch by this means; our many attempts to abolish given evils will necessarily remain a treatment of symptoms, leaving the deepest causes of unhealth untouched because intellectual discern-ment, the essential diagnosis, is wanting. Fundamentally, religion is concerned with such a diagnosis, and, in the light of it, with the remedies to be applied; it is directly concerned with nothing else.

While we are on the subject of cosmology, something must be said about the theory of cosmic cycles, highly developed in Indian tradition but also known to Western antiquity with its golden, silver, bronze, and iron ages, the first-named corresponding to a period of primordial purity, of which the terrestrial paradise gives the type, the lattermost indicating a period of general obscurity due to the neglect or loss of the essential knowledge, leading to a catastrophe that will appear to the humanity concerned as a final discrimination or judgement. When one considers the process of cosmic development in relation to human existence, individual and collective, it is apparent that there are times and occasions when a kind of cumulative bias in one or other direction takes place, like a spring or neap tide which nevertheless leaves the ocean itself essentially as it was. In a minor way recorded history is full of examples of this kind; but it is possible also to recognise oscillations on a much larger scale in which the tendency toward enlightenment or toward infatuation becomes so pronounced as to justify the use of the broader classification of cyclic phases mentioned above. Each of these great divisions of time represents a piling up of positive or negative factors which the beings who experience the results will interpret in terms of quasi-universal good or evil, though in point of fact the process of cosmic flux goes on uninterruptedly, nothing of this world being intrinsically permanent or satisfying. For man to seek his real home amid these ever-shifting quicksands seems like asking for disappointment; and yet this is precisely where his quest must start – from the very situation, that is to say, determined for him by antecedent karma, which he has the power neither to choose nor to refuse. The gate of deliverance can be found only here and now, not elsewhere or otherwhen.

By now enough will have been said to show that if there be a question that urgently concerns us – the word 'problem' was unhappy – it is neither the existence of the world nor our idea of what a world might have been like had we been asked to create one, but solely the question of how best to rejoin our own centre, which is also the centre of all things, the Tree of Life, the axis uniting heaven and earth. The word 'religion' by its derivation means 'to unite', and so does the word 'yoga' – the same root as 'yoke'.

In effect we have somehow to retrace the steps of our forefather Adam, but in inverse order. For him it was an outgoing path that lured him from centre to periphery, a consequence of the illusory duplication of the original unity, whereby the Tree of Life became mysteriously clothed in the semblance of the Tree of Good and Evil; this gives us the very pattern and principle of distraction in this world.

For the posterity of Adam, nourished as we are day after day on the fruits, white or black, of the dualistic tree, the process of return must start out from here, as was said once before, which means that it is the Tree of Good and Evil this time that must be caused to yield up its secret by revealing its identity with the Tree of Life, even while remaining itself at its own level.

This brings us to the point where it is possible to speak of *realisation in active mode*, which we promised to discuss when speaking of the Adamic innocence. This innocence is always a perfection in its own way, like that of the newly born – hence the injunction to enter the Kingdom as a little child – but its existential passivity leaves it vulnerable to the egocentric urge that lets men feel themselves 'as gods' and places them under the law of mortality by that very fact. For unequivocal liberation it needs to be completed by the active realisation, full awareness of the essential identity, across their relative distinction, of the Tree of Life and the Tree of Contrast, nirvana and samsāra. It is only this transcending of all the dualities and their oppositions that can render one immune to the serpent's stinging, because then the serpent itself, like everything else, will in the light of knowledge have been recognised for what it is, namely a property of existence and no more. Light therefore takes priority among all our needs; the Buddha in placing 'right view' at the beginning of the Noble Eightfold Path that leads to deliverance paid full tribute to this first requirement. Though passive and active realisation have both been mentioned in turn, it is necessary to make a third point by saying that reintegration in the centre, to be complete and in balance, will in fact be active and passive at one and the same time, the former in virtue of knowledge that is active by its own nature like the intellect that communicates it, and the latter in virtue of the living gift of grace, the spontaneous attraction of the centre itself, which cannot be commanded but can only be accepted freely or else ignored; in which case, as Schuon said in one of his most telling passages, it is always man who is absent, not grace. To follow the spiritual way, the ingoing path, a two-directional traffic will therefore always be implied, whatever may be the apparent emphasis in any given case, as between human initiative on the one hand and divine gift on the other; it is the very disproportion between a necessarily limited human effort, however intense, and the transcendent and unlimited object to be encompassed that shows why this must be so.

The traditional image of the Buddha – perhaps the most miraculous form of icon in existence – perfectly exemplifies the synthesis of attitudes required of man by the circumstances. As he sits in lotus posture at the foot of the Tree of Enlightenment – the Tree of Life it might just as well be called – the Buddha, the fully awakened, touches with his right hand the earth, calling her to witness; an active attitude toward 'the world' is indicated by this gesture. His left hand, for its part, supports the begging-bowl held in readiness to receive whatever may be cast into it from above; this gesture indicates passivity toward heaven, perfect receptiveness. The incomparable eloquence of this symbol beggars all comment.

For a Christian, the realisation in active mode is represented essentially by the redemption inaugurated by Christ Himself. To compensate for the fall, the path of reintegration has to pass through the sacrifice – the ego must suffer transformation in the fire of Shiva, as a Hindu would put it. Virtual reintegration into the Adamic state of innocence, in passive mode, is operated through baptism. Virtual reintegration in active mode, into the Christic state, is operated through the Eucharist, the eating and drinking of Christ in order to be eaten and drunk by Christ. Herein is to be seen all the difference separating 'the sinner that repenteth' from 'the just person that needs no repentance'. It is the former that corresponds to the active realisation: the bird that has escaped from the cage will never again be caught. The innocence represented by the passive participation is indubitable, but it is the other that calls forth the greatest joy in heaven.

Incidentally, the foregoing citation provides an excellent illustration of the polyvalent character of revealed Scripture, in virtue of which the same words, while retaining their literal applicability at one level of understanding, are transposable into a more universal sense at another. Here is a case of that method of exegesis referred to once before under the name of 'anagogical', as pointing upward to the threshold of the mysteries. The immense stress laid by all the great traditions on scriptural memorising and recitation is explained by this property of the sacred text to vehicle superposed aspects of the truth, whereby it is able to provide a support for meditation and concentration that is practically inexhaustible.

This twofold virtuality, covering all possibilities both passive and active, has to be *actualised* through the life in religion; religious doctrines and methods, whatever their particularity of form, have no other purpose but this.

Moreover, the same is the unique purpose of human life as such – 'human life hard to obtain', as the Buddhists say, and therefore not to be frittered away in irrelevant, profane pursuits. Again and again the various traditional paths rejoin one another in this urgent plea to man to fulfil his human destiny, which is none other than deliverance – or salvation, if the Christian term be preferred, always provided it is given the sense not of some individualistic compromise or other but that given it by Christ's own words when he said, 'Be ye perfect even as your Father in Heaven is perfect', surely the most awe-inspiring injunction to be found in Scripture.

The transcendent nature of the human vocation and of its finality is evidenced, above all, by the presence, in man, of a sense of the Absolute. The name of God is indelibly inscribed in the human heart; all the profane overlayings due to inattention and consequent ignorance are unable quite to extinguish its remembrance, though they may at times come near to doing so in practice. Even man's infidelities betray themselves by their inconsistency. As Meister Eckhardt put it, 'The more he blasphemes the more he praises God.' At any degree, the state of forgetfulness will always carry with it a gnawing sense of privation, which will not be stilled until its one real object, instead of many fancied ones, has been found again. Did we but know it, all the desires beings experience, all their attempts to snatch satisfaction from this thing or that thing, are but signs of a deep-seated homesickness for the Tree of Life, man's true homeland.

The one and only 'problem', in our situation, is to find the way home, in which case we can show it to others. One who has missed his own way makes a poor guide; to have ignored this fact is what vitiates so much so-called service in the world, a typically humanitarian delusion. In the long run, only the saints can offer efficient service, those who know the way by walking it.

The way itself involves two conditions, namely a direction – the sacred tradition provides this direction – and a method of concentration appropriate to each person's relative capacity; but whatever form this may take in practice, in principle method is reducible to the unbroken remembrance of God, perfect mindfulness in the Buddhist sense. The Prophet of Islam, speaking with the fierce eloquence of the desert, has cried out: 'All in the world is accursed except the Remembrance of God.' Whatever is attachable to that remembrance is acceptable; whatever is incompatible is for rejection. This is the law governing the whole spiritual enterprise.

Man is human by his vocation; he is subhuman in proportion as he disregards it. The animals and plants who follow their own destiny are superior to the man who betrays his. To spend the precious gift of human existence on anything but 'the one thing needful', as Christ described it while in the house of Martha and Mary, is to condemn oneself to the fate of the Flying Dutchman and sail the ocean of existence interminably to and fro, buffeted by its gales and deluded by its calms while always seeking a haven. Divine grace always leaves us this one hope; God who now seems so distant is ever close at hand – 'closer than your jugular vein', as the Koran has it. The Tree of Life is standing in this room, as certainly as it stood in Eden; it is a pity if we will not use our eyes.

IV

Is There Room for 'Grace' in Buddhism?

To the question 'Is there room for grace in Buddhism?' there are many today who without further reflection would give a negative reply. It is a commonplace of neo-Buddhist apologetics with an eye on the fashionable 'humanism' of the Western world to stress both the exclusively self-directed achievement of the Buddha as 'discoverer' of the way to enlightenment and also, on the strength of the Buddha's example, the purely empirical character of the opportunity open to those who would follow in his footsteps. Within its proper traditional context the first of these two statements is valid, whereas the second one rests on more doubtful grounds and certainly needs qualifying in several important respects. However, it can be admitted that a perspective that does not include the idea of a personal God may seem, at first sight, to leave little room for the idea of grace either. How could a merciful action from above, definable in terms of an unsolicited gift offered to men independently of their own effort, be reconciled, so some will argue, with the inflexible dispensation ascribed to the manifested universe itself, as expressed in the doctrine of concordant action and reaction, karma and its fruits? Yet this idea of 'grace', which translates a divine function, is by no means unintelligible in the light of Buddhist teachings, being in fact implicit in every known form of spirituality, the Buddhist form included. The question, however, is how to situate the said idea in a manner that implies no contradiction, since it must be freely admitted that the Buddhist wisdom has not given to the idea of grace the same form as it has received in the personalist and theistic doctrines of· Semitic provenance; nor is such a thing to be expected, inasmuch as the 'economy' of the respective traditions rests on very different premises, thus affecting both doctrines and the manner of their application in practice. Each kind of wisdom determines the nature of its corresponding method. Buddhism has always made of this a governing principle of spiritual life at any degree or level.

Evidently the nature of the Christic revelation was such as to require a strong affirmation of the element of grace from the very outset, which was not the case with Buddhism. Such differences in the line of approach to the saving truth are in the nature of things and should cause no surprise given the diversifying of mankind in the course of its karmic development. The important thing to recognise in this case is the fact that the word 'grace' corresponds to a whole dimension of spiritual experience; it is unthinkable that this should be absent from one of the great religions of the world. In fact, anyone who has lived in a traditionally Buddhist country knows that this dimension finds its expression there too, vehicled by the appropriate forms. For us it is of interest to observe these forms and clarify for ourselves the teaching they carry explicitly or else latently. The present essay should be regarded as contributing to this clarification.

The pursuit of enlightenment, which is the purpose for which Buddhism exists, is paradoxical by its own showing inasmuch as this aim appears to require an encompassing of the greater by the less, of the imperishable by the ephemeral, of absolute knowledge by a relative ignorance; it seems to make of man the subject and of enlightenment the object of the quest. Moreover, a similar paradox applies in the theistic forms of religion; people speak of seeking God and of contemplating his perfections even while knowing that in terms of human measurement and however far along the road a man may have proceeded, God lies farther still and that no unilaterally directed human perception or effort is adequate to the divine truth even across one of its aspects, to say nothing of its essence. In Buddhist terms no human powers however stretched can possibly match up to the suchness of enlightenment. Yet Buddhahood, to which we are invited by the teaching and tradition of the Buddha and still more by his example, is just this. Nothing less is offered to us, since it is axiomatic to the Buddhist revelation as such that to reach this transcendent goal does, in principle, lie within the scope of every human being in virtue of that being's place on the axis of Buddhahood – for this is what to be human really means – and also, more indirectly, within the scope of every being whatsoever 'down to the last blade of grass', as the saying goes, via the prior attainment of a human birth in this world or, if another world be in question, a birth of corresponding centrality.

For a start, it is worth pointing out that, if from the non-personalist standpoint of Buddhism the supreme goal is presented as 'a state' (hence the use of a word like 'enlightenment'), from the standpoint of the Semitic religions that goal is most commonly clothed in the attributes of personality. Nevertheless in the latter religions the word 'God' will always comprise, be it more or less unconsciously, the idea of the unqualifiable *Godhead*, and this is true even when the word is being quite loosely used. Despite the antimetaphysical bias of much Western theological thinking, it would be a mistake to conclude that the qualifying of God as 'person' constitutes a limit in principle. In Islam this particular danger of confusion is in practice less marked than in Christianity. Outside the Semitic world, Hinduism reconciles the two points of view, personal and impersonal, with perfect ease.

Where Buddhism is concerned, despite its preference for impersonal expressions, one could yet ask oneself 'Whose is the state of enlightenment?' since the word itself, as used, does not altogether keep clear of anthropomorphic overtones; neither does one speak of Buddha, once enlightened, as 'It' – all of which goes to prove that in this sphere, as in others, it is not the words used but the manner of using them in a given context that counts. Both modes of expression, the personal as well as the impersonal, are possible and therefore legitimate, since each may serve as an *upāya*, or provisional means, for the purpose of evoking, rather than defining, a reality that is inexpressible in terms of our earthly experience. Provided it has this effect on those for whom it is intended, the means in question becomes acceptable. Given our common human condition as thinking and talking animals, there is no reason to fight shy of a more or less anthropomorphic terminology when discussing even the most sublime of subjects provided one does not forget the truth that if speech is good, speech nevertheless arises from the rupture of a silence which is better still. 'The Buddha's silence' regarding the nature of the Ultimate is, among his many and various *upāyas*, the most enlightening of all. When the Buddha spoke no word but merely held up a flower, Zen took birth; there is a profound lesson in this story.

Fortified by this precaution, it is now possible to approach our chosen theme by quoting a famous passage from the Pali Canon (*Udana* 7:1–3) wherein lies concealed a key to the understanding of what 'grace' means in a Buddhist setting. Here is the passage in question:

> There is, O monks, an unborn, an unbecome, an unmade, an uncompounded; if, O monks, there were not here this unborn, unbecome, unmade, uncompounded, there would not here be an escape from the born, the become, the made, the compounded. But because there is an unborn, an unbecome, an unmade, an uncompounded, therefore there is an escape from the born, the become, the made, the compounded.

The above quotation is plainly couched in the language of transcendence; any Christian or Muslim could have used these same words when referring to God and the world. This transcendence is propounded by the sutra as providing real grounds for human hope. What it does not do, however, is to define the link between the two terms under comparison; we still need to be shown the bridge over which changefulness must pass to reach the eternal. This link or bridge in fact corresponds to that very function of divine grace that is the object of our present investigation.

The key to the problem lies in a property of transcendence itself. Given the incommensurable gap apparently fixed between enlightenment and the seeker after enlightenment – ignorant by definition – it is self-evident to anyone who thinks at all, and still more so to anyone possessed of a metaphysical flair, that such a seeking on the part of a human being with his necessarily imperfect vision and limited powers does not really make sense when taken at its face value alone. Enlightenment (or God for that matter) cannot possibly be situated at the passive pole in relation to man's endeavour, it cannot *per se* become object to man as subject. If our human language sometimes makes things seem so, it is high time we became aware of its inadequacy. Buddhism for its part will add that here is patent evidence of the illusory character of the human claim to selfhood, to which all our conceptual aberrations are severally and collectively imputable.

To put the above argument somewhat differently, man cannot possibly be the active agent in an operation wherein enlightenment plays the passive part. Whatever may or may not be suggested by appearances, the truth has to be read the other way round, since enlightenment, awareness of the divine reality, belongs outside all becoming by definition; it is wholly 'in act', so that wherever one discerns contingency or potentiality, as in the case of our human seeking, this of necessity pertains to samsāra, to the changing, the impermanent, the compounded. It is this very character of potentiality, experienceable positively as arising and negatively as subsiding, which makes samsāra, the Round of Existence, to be such as it is.

The consequences of the above observation are momentous; for, if there is to be a wooing of enlightenment by man, it is nevertheless the former that, in principle and in fact, remains the real subject of the quest as well as its ostensible object. It has often been said that in enlightenment the subject–object distinction is cancelled out – a truth to bear in mind even if, in our present state, this remains more of a puzzling thought than a verified reality. Metaphysical intuition, however, already allows one to know – or shall we say, to sense – that intrinsically enlightenment is the active factor in our situation and that it is man who, for all his apparent initiative and effort represents the passive term of the supreme adequation. Meister Eckhardt puts this whole question into proper perspective when he says that 'in the course of nature it is really the higher which is ever more ready to pour out its power into the lower than the lower is ready to receive it' for as he goes on to say, 'there is no dearth of God with us; what dearth there is is wholly ours who make not ready to receive his grace'. Where he said 'God', you have but to say 'enlightenment', and the result will be a Buddhist statement in form as well as content.

The great paradox, for us, is that we still cannot help viewing this situation in reverse; a misplaced egocentricity makes us do so: we all have to suffer the congenital illusion of existence in which every creature as yet undelivered shares in greater or lesser degree. Buddhism invites us to get this thing straight in the first place, prior to showing us that the two viewpoints on reality, the relative and absolute, samsāra and nirvana, essentially coincide, as the Heart Sutra explicitly teaches.

In China the Taoists have always spoken of the 'activity of

heaven'; for us to speak of the 'activity of enlightenment' is in no wise far-fetched. This is in fact the function of grace, namely to condition men's homecoming to the centre from start to finish. It is the very attraction of the centre itself, revealed to us by various means, which provides the incentive to start on the way and the energy to face and overcome its many and various obstacles. Likewise grace is the welcoming hand into the centre when man finds himself standing at long last on the brink of the great divide where all familiar human landmarks have disappeared. Only he who came down from heaven can ascend to heaven, as the Gospel says, but about this mystery it is useless for ignorance to speculate, let alone speak. Till the great leap in the dark is taken, faith in the Buddha's enlightenment must be our lamp, since all that stems from light is light, and even our darkness, did we but know it, is none other than the dazzlement inflicted by a radiance too intense for samsaric eyes to bear.

The attractive influence of enlightenment, experienced as providential and merciful emanation from the luminous centre, strikes on human consciousness in three ways, which might be described respectively as: (1) invitation into enlightenment, (2) companionship of enlightenment, and (3) reminders of enlightenment.

The first-named corresponds to 'conversion', the gift of faith. The second corresponds to man's being 'in a state of grace', in virtue of which his apparent weakness is enabled to envisage tasks and surmount obstacles far beyond ordinary human strength. The third way coincides with the supplying of various 'means of grace', that is to say *upāyas* consecrated by tradition – scriptural teachings, methods of meditation, initiatic rites and the like. Moreover, the whole inspiration of an art properly describable as 'sacred' issues from this source. In short, whatever serves as a reminder of enlightenment or helps to keep attention in that line of vision is a 'means of grace' in the sense here intended. It is worth dwelling on the above three factors of attraction in somewhat greater detail.

Invitation into enlightenment. This phrase has been coined by way of describing a man's first clear experiencing of an overriding call to turn his religious life into a reality. Antecedent circumstances, such as a person's background formation or the degree of his or her intellectual maturity, need not be taken into account in the present instance; all one is concerned with is the nature of the event itself.

Until 'the thought of enlightenment' (*bodhi-citta*) has gained a place in one's consciousness, one can hardly claim to be 'travelling' in a Buddhist sense. The awakening of faith remains a great mystery; its negative concomitant will always be a certain turning away from the world, and it is only later (save by rare exception) that any question of integrating the world positively, in the sense of the essential identity of samsāra and nirvana as expressed in the Heart Sutra (this was mentioned before), can play an effective part in one's preoccupations. 'Non-duality' is not for the beginner; presented as an abstract theory, this idea can even be harmful for a mind insufficiently prepared because it leads only too easily to pretensions of an ego-inflating kind – hence the danger of much that passes for Zen or Vedanta today. The extreme reticence of some religious groups on the subject, which it is the fashion to blame, is by no means unjustified in the light of results.

An important thing to notice here is that the sense of spiritual urgency, whether coming to a person suddenly or else by hardly perceptible steps, is experienced as a call to activity whereof the person himself is in the first place the passive recipient, having done nothing particular to bring it about; this is typical and normal and admirably fits in with the description of a grace as being 'free gift'. All at once a peremptory urge takes root in that man's soul telling him that enlightenment is the only thing of worth in its own right and that all other things, be they great or small, can only be properly valued in proportion as they contribute to that end or else impede its attainment. Once this has happened, the essentials of spiritual life are there, namely discernment between the real and the illusory and the will to concentrate upon the real; this latter definition comes from Frithjof Schuon. However elementary may be one's present awareness of this twofold call, whereof wisdom and method are the respective expressions, it can be said with certainty that a foretaste of enlightenment has been received; it is as if a ray spontaneously emitted from the centre has come in to effect a first incision in the shell of human ignorance because the Buddha-nature in a man wishes to be delivered. More than this cannot be said about something that baffles all the calculations of the ordinary mind.

Companionship of enlightenment. If invitation into the Way is something of a unique event in a human life, the graces to be experienced in the course of following that way are multiple in the sense that they repeat that first call at various stages of spiritual development in the form of an urge to proceed further, to deepen this experience or that, to eliminate such and such causes of distraction, or to concentrate on this or that aspect of awareness. This process can be illustrated by comparing it to the climbing of some mountain ridge leading to a summit. At the start of the ascent the thought of the summit alone possesses one's mind, but when once one is actually on the ridge each successive pinnacle or gash needing to be surmounted will engage all one's attention to the point of temporarily eclipsing remembrance of the summit itself. The nearer obstacles do in fact continue to reveal the existence of the summit by implication, but also in a sense they veil it; in other words, each obstacle in turn serves to symbolise the summit and thus becomes a factor of awareness in a relative sense. Thus do the things encountered in samsaric existence prove the latent presence of enlightenment even while appearing to hide it. A 'symbol' is a key to knowledge; an 'idol' is a symbol taken for a reality in its own right. This is a fundamental distinction to bear in mind, because symbolism, properly understood and applied, is the very stuff of the spiritual alchemy whereby the samsaric lead may be transmitted into the Buddhic gold it is in principle. In all this process, be the way long or short, the companionship of enlightenment is operating like a ferment, an ever-present grace filling the gap, as it were, between our human incapacity and the apparently superhuman task to which we are committed thanks to a human birth.

Seeing that the Way with its stages has just been mentioned in correlation with the effusion of grace, this will provide an opportunity to discuss one question that has often been a cause of confusion, namely how we are to situate our own present life in the general scheme of transmigration as set forth by Buddhism. For this purpose a brief digression will not come amiss.

The question might be put this way: When considering the path to enlightenment, are we to take into account, as some might ask, the extended possibilities implied in successive births (sometimes reckoned by the million), or should we confine our attention to present existence while ignoring the rest except in the sense of a more or less schematic representation of saṃsāra, the world's flow, as conditioned by the continual interplay of action and reaction, karma and its fruits? This is indeed a pertinent question to put, since it touches something quite fundamental in Buddhism, namely the truth that to know samsāra's true nature is to know nirvana, nothing less. The converse also holds good; for, if one may be allowed to paraphrase a sentence of Saint Thomas Aquinas, 'A false opinion concerning the world will fatally engender a false opinion concerning enlightenment' (Saint Thomas says 'concerning God'), the two awarenesses hang together as a single reality.

Coming as a fresh and unfamiliar idea, transmigration often makes a strong appeal to a Western mind just because it seems to provide for 'a second chance', that is to say for the possibility of taking the way to enlightenment by easy stages instead of having to stake one's all on a single throw, as the Semitic eschatologies would appear to suggest. For one who takes this complacent view of his human opportunities, it is only too easy to read into the doctrine of samsaric rebirth something closely akin to the current belief in a one-directional 'progress'; whether this belief be clothed in the more scientific-sounding phraseology of 'evolution' on Teilhardian lines or otherwise makes no matter.

Evidently such a view disagrees with Buddhism inasmuch as it misses the chief point about transmigration, namely its essential *indefinitude* – this can never be said too often – as also, incidentally, the high degree of improbability attaching to any kind of human rebirth when weighed up in terms of karmic consequence. It is not very logical (to say the least of it) to spend most of one's earthly life in the pursuit not of enlightenment but of all that is unnecessary and trivial and then to expect this life to repeat itself in human form; yet this is precisely the life led by a majority of people and not least by those whom the world regards as highly civilised and admires for their manipulative dexterity or their insatiable erudition. What right have these people to expect privileged treatment when the time comes for them to be weighed on the karmic scales? Have they ever given a thought to that saying about 'human birth hard to obtain' which runs through Buddhism like a refrain? If one wishes to be honest with oneself, one has to admit that in most cases rebirth as a worm would be a merciful requital; certainly one is being less than prudent if one assumes that the hells of Buddhism are only there to accommodate murderers and gangsters. How many of us would ever have the nerve to commit murder? To what kind of rebirth, then, is it likely that a frittered consciousness will lead, or a persistent lukewarmness in respect of truth?

The Semitic eschatologies, which offer man the single alternative 'salvation or perdition', can at least claim an empirical realism for this narrowing of choice on the grounds that such an attitude makes for a sense of urgency in life and is therefore, spiritually speaking, an *upāya* adjusted to its purpose. For the Buddhist, what in fact replaces the Christian's fear of God's wrath is the fear of interminable wandering through samsāra, now up, now down, but never free from suffering. Any attempt to read into the samsaric process an idea of something like a uniform cosmic movement endowed with an optimistic trend is as un-Buddhist as it is improbable in itself.

In point of fact, whenever enlightenment is attained, this is always from the vantage point of a particular human life, or an equivalent state if another world system be in question; the individual called Prince Siddhartha who became Sakya Muni Buddha perfectly illustrates the above statement. One must not slip into thinking of enlightenment as if it were the last and sweetest of a long-drawn-out harvest of samsaric fruits. Good karma, any life well spent, contributes to one's enlightenment, first because virtue is dispositive to knowledge while vice does the reverse and second because within the scale of samsaric possibilities good karma promotes the emergence of fresh creations in relatively favourable surroundings as, for instance, in countries where enlightenment is not forgotten, which is no small advantage in this world. To this extent a life well and intelligently spent is not irrelevant to one's attainment of the goal, even if one stops short somewhere on the path. To admit this is, however, very different from turning this possibility of good karma into an excuse for postponing one's best efforts till a future life assumed to be better than the present one. This very attitude almost makes it certain that it will be worse. In any case, so long as one remains a samsaric being, any kind of relapse is possible; it is salutary to bear this in mind while putting all one's effort into immediate opportunities consonantly with present grace. Above all it should be remembered that enlightenment, if and when it comes, spells a reversal of all samsaric values or, in a still deeper sense, their integration. If it be currently said of a Buddha that 'he knows all his anterior births', this is because he is identified with the heart of causality, the mysterious hub of the wheel of becoming where no motion ever was or could be. Beings still in samsāra do not enjoy this possibility, so that it would seem in every way more practical for them to make the best of a human opportunity while they have it, instead of banking on a future that could be anything from a paradise of devas to an infernal sojourn amid fire or ice.

A most important thing to remember in all this is that the attainer of enlightenment is not 'this man so-and-so' but rather that it is by the ending of the dream of one's own 'so-and-so ness' that enlightenment arises. As far as knowledge of samsāra is concerned, what is needed is for each thing to be put in its own place, neither plus nor minus, including one's own person. When all things have become transparent to the point of allowing the Uncreated Light to shine right through them, there is nothing further to become. Becoming is the continual process of resolving internal contradictions, fruits of the dualistic tree, by means of partial compensations leading to fresh contradictions and so on indefinitely. To understand this process with full clarity is to escape its domination. The Buddha has shown the way.

With this question behind us, let us take up the last of our three headings, *reminders of enlightenment*, but this need not long detain us; it is enough to have listed a certain number of type examples of 'means of grace' as supplied by the tradition under various forms and in view of various uses. All traditional civilisations abound in such reminders; once one is aware that such exist, it is easy to observe the workings of grace through the medium of these forms. Nevertheless, there remains one example that deserves quite special attention as a supreme reminder and means of grace: this is the sacramental image of the Blessed One found in every corner of the Buddhist world. We will take up this subject in due course.

The next channelling of grace to be offered to the reader's attention is one that takes us into a spiritual dimension close to the heart of things. This is the function of guru, or spiritual master, of him who initiates a man into the path that leads via the higher states of consciousness to the threshold of enlightenment itself – so near and yet so far, since the final passage remains pure mystery whereof grace alone holds the key. In a very special sense the spiritual master is the representative of 'the spirit that bloweth where it listeth'. His qualification for such an office devolves on him outside any determinable test. If he be not yet discovered, his very seeking confers light; when found, his favour may yet be granted or withheld without any reasons given. His displeasure is the bitterest medicine for any man to swallow. In his master's presence the disciple is expected to behave as if the Buddha himself stood before him; in the Christian initiation centred on the Jesus Prayer the same advice is given, with substitution of the person of Christ.

In relation to the Sangha the guru stands for its essence; this is true even if the master be not himself a bhikku, though obviously he often is that too. The famous guru of Mila Repa, Marpa, was a consecrated layman with a family, than whom no greater master has existed anywhere; just as in the matter of discipleship Mila Repa is unsurpassed, to say the least of it. His own poems, the most beautiful in the Tibetan language, ring of the guru's grace at every turn, even though as far as personal effort is concerned Mila Repa's persistence in the face of Marpa's calculated (but ever so compassionate) snubbing is something so unheard of as to make one think that a man must be born a Tibetan to stay such a course.

However, the human guru is not the whole story; there is another guru to be considered, interior this time and whose visible counterpart the outward guru is. 'Intellect' is his name, Socrates's *daemon*; it is unfortunate that later usage has debased a word that by rights should be confined to the intuitive intelligence indwelling at the heart of every being and especially of man, the immanent grace about which Christ said 'the Kingdom of Heaven is within you'. When the outer guru has done his work, he hands over to the inner guru, leaving him to do the rest.

Intellect can save us because it is that in us which needs no saving, seeing that enlightenment is in its very substance. Stemming from light, itself is light, leading back to light. The great puzzle is our egotism, our false sense of selfhood and consequent reluctance to let go what never makes us really happy. Our recurring dissatisfactions are also guru; all we have to do is to trace these dissatisfactions to their primary cause. This is the positive message of suffering, a message that also harbours a hope, one that surely cannot forever remain unheeded. The Buddha's 'First Truth' really teaches nothing different.

Let us now take a brief flight out of this suffering world in order to visit the homeland of grace and the source of its bountiful stream. Mahayana Buddhism speaks of three *kayas*, or bodies of Buddhahood, or, if one so prefers, three mansions of enlightenment considered respectively as essence or suchness, fruition or bliss, and avataric projection into the world; the corresponding Sanskrit names are *Dharma-kaya*, *Sambboga-kaya*, and *Nirmana-kaya*, and it is especially of this third body that something must now be said, as relating directly to the question of grace and its manifestation among beings.

A quotation from a short but highly concentrated Tibetan sutra composed in verse, *The Good Wish of Great Power*, will provide us with the essential data: 'Uninterruptedly my avataras [incarnations] will appear in inconceivable millions and will show forth various means for the conversion of every kind of being. Through the prayer of my compassion may all sentient beings of the three spheres be delivered from the six samsāric abodes.'

Traditionally, the 'revealer' of this sutra is given as the Buddha Samanta Bhadra, the 'All Good'; significantly his name is preceded by the prefix Adi – or primordial – thus stressing the principial nature of the attribution. Concerning the primordial reality whereof this Buddha is spokesman, it is also said that neither the name of *nirvāna* nor of *samsāra* applies to it, for it is pure 'non-duality' (*advaita*) beyond all possible distinction or expression. To realise this truth fully is to be *buddha*, awake; not to realise it is to wander in samsaric existence; the sutra says this expressly.

In their ceaseless warfare waged against men's proneness to superimpose their own concepts on the Divinity as such, the Buddhist sutras have introduced the word 'void' to suggest the total absence of positive or negative definability; hence also the Buddha's title of Shunya-murti, 'Form of the Void' – a contradiction in terms that again serves to underline a truth that eludes all attempts at positive enunciation.

As soon as one passes over to attribution, by saying of divinity that 'it is' or 'is not' this or that or else by giving names such as 'all good', etc., one is perforce in the realm of being; the merciful epithet mentioned above is, among names, one of the first to impose itself. The visible sign of this merciful presence is to be seen in the stream of avataric revelation (hence the use of the word 'millions' in the sutra), the Buddhas and Bodhisattvas who appear in the various world systems and, through their own enlightenment, show the way of deliverance to creatures. Our sutra concludes with the following words: 'May beings of the three spheres one and all by the prayer of my contemplation ... finally attain Buddhahood.'

This grants the very charter of grace and of its operation in the world; it hardly calls for further comment.

All that can usefully be added is perhaps to point out that if, in Christianity for example, the aspect of 'Divine Personality' may sometimes seem to have obscured the Suchness of the Godhead itself, in the case of Buddhism, though this danger has been sedulously avoided, a certain personal expression of the Divine is nevertheless to be found there in 'distributive' form, namely as the heavenly company or sangha of Buddhas and Bodhisattvas, with the former standing for its static and the latter for its dynamic aspect, as mercy when projected into samsāra itself. In the final section of this essay, when the Pure Land doctrine is discussed, this question will be taken up again.

After this excursion to the heights we must come down to earth again and examine one concrete means of grace, mentioned before, which perhaps more than all others has helped to keep remembrance of enlightenment alive among men. This is the image of the Buddha making the 'earth-touching' (*bhumi-sparsha*) gesture. Every corner of the Buddhist world knows and loves this image; both Theravada and Mahayana have produced marvellous examples of it. If there be a symbolical representation to which the word 'miraculous' properly applies, this surely is the one.

The story of how a Buddha image came to exist at all is instructive, since Buddhism at the beginning did not incline to anthropomorphic imagery, preferring more elementary symbols. It is said that several abortive attempts were made to put the Buddha's likeness on record from motives of a personal kind, such as the wish to remember a loved and revered figure and so on; a certain confusing of appearance and reality is always involved in such cases, hence the prohibition of the 'graven image' by Judaism and Islam, for instance. However, in this case the compassion of the Victorious One intervened; he was prepared to allow an image of himself provided this was a true symbol and not a mere reproduction of surfaces – this distinction is very important. Yielding to his devotees' prayers, the Buddha projected his own form miraculously and it was this projection that provided the model for a true icon, fit to serve a purpose other than that of personal adulation such as a sacred theme by definition precludes.

I should like to quote here from *Sacred Art in East and West*, by Titus Burckhardt, in which a whole chapter is devoted to the traditional Buddha-*rupa*. After mentioning the above story about the frustration of the artists and the miraculous projection, the author continues:

> . . . the sacred ikon is a manifestation of the grace of the Buddha, it emanates from his supra-human power. . . . If one considers the matter fully one can see that the two aspects of Buddhism, the doctrine of karma and its quality of grace, are inseparable, for to demonstrate the real nature of the world is to transcend it; it is to manifest the changeless states . . . and it is a breach made in the closed system of becoming. This breach is the Buddha himself; thenceforth all that comes from him carries the influx of *Bodhi*.

The enlightening function of the sacred image could not have been better put.

Before going into the various details of the image itself, it were well to refresh our memory about the episode in the Buddha's life which this particular posture is meant to perpetuate. Everyone will remember that shortly before his enlightenment the Buddha-to-be proceeded into the great primeval forest near the place in Bihar now called Bodh-gaya and there found a spreading pipal tree (*Ficus religiosa*) at the foot of which a seat stood ready prepared for one destined to become the Light of the World; the tree itself obviously stands for the world's axis, the Tree of Life, as Genesis calls it. Just as he was about to take his seat there, Mara the tempter appeared before him, challenging his right to the adamantine throne. 'I am prince of this world,' Mara said, 'so the throne belongs to me.' Then the Bodhisattva stretched forth his right hand and touched the earth, mother of all creatures, calling on her to witness that the throne was his by right, and earth testified that this was so.

In the classical form of this image the Buddha is always shown sitting upon a lotus; choice of this water plant is in itself significant inasmuch as in the traditional lore 'the waters' always symbolise existence with its teeming possibilities, that samsāra which the Buddha was to show the way to overcome, not by mere denial but by showing forth its true nature. As for the figure itself, its right hand points downward to touch the earth as in the story while its left hand is turned upward to support the begging bowl, sign of a bhikku's estate. Just as the bhikku in his bowl catches whatever the passer-by may choose to cast into it, be it much or little, not asking for more but letting it serve his own sustenance for the day, so also man has to accept the heavenly grace as the free gift it is. In the two gestures displayed by the Buddha image the whole programme of man's spiritual exigencies is summed up.

Toward the earth, that is to say toward the world to which he belongs by his existence, man's gesture is *active*; such an active attitude is always needed where the world and its manifold temptations and distractions are concerned. Toward heaven and its gifts, on the other hand, the spiritual man is *passive*, he is content to receive the dew of grace as and when it falls and to refresh his more or less flagging powers with its aid. As for the ignorant man, he does just the reverse, showing himself soft and accommodating toward the world while making all kinds of conditions of his own choosing where the things of heaven are concerned, if indeed he deigns to give them any thought at all. For the truly mindful man, even his own karma can be both grace and guru, not merely in the sense of reward or sanction imposed by a cosmic law, but because karma is a potent and inescapable reminder of enlightenment as the crying need of man and as the only unequivocably reasonable object of his desires. Accepted in this sense, karma, be it good or evil, can be welcomed as Savitri once welcomed Death when he came to claim her husband and by her resignation overcame him. Contemplated rightly, the Buddha's sacramental image tells us all these things. For us, it is the means of grace *par excellence*.

Sufficient has by now been said (or so one hopes) by way of answering our original question as to whether Buddhism leaves any room for grace. One last illustration, however, will serve to clinch the argument by showing that the idea of grace can play a predominant part in a doctrine that nonetheless remains Buddhist in both form and flavour. This is the Pure Land doctrine (*Jōdō* in Japanese), developed around the vow of the Buddha Amitabha and using, for its single operative means, the invocation of his name. The name itself means 'Infinite Light' and the Buddha thus denoted is the one who presides over the Western quarter, where his own 'Buddha-land' is symbolically situated. It must be mentioned, in passing, that Europeans who feel drawn to Buddhism have hitherto been inclined to avoid the Pure Land form of it just because of its insistence on grace, described there as *tariki* (other power), which reminded them too much of the Christianity they believed themselves to have left behind. Western seekers have on the whole felt more drawn to *jiriki* (own power) methods, those where personal initiative and heroic effort are greatly stressed – hence their preference for Zen (or what they take for such) or else Theravada interpreted in an ultrapuritanical, not to say humanistic, sense; not for anything would these people be mistaken for miserable, God-dependent Christians! I hope, however, to show that the two lines of approach, *jiriki* and *tariki*, are by no means as incompatible as some affect to believe and that, despite contrasts of emphasis, the two belong together and are in fact indispensable to one another.

Taking Zen first, one thing that many of its foreign admirers are apt to lose sight of is the fact that, in its own country, those who feel called into that way will already, since childhood, have been moulded by the strict discipline of Japanese tradition in which respect for authority, an elaborate civility, and the acceptance of many formal restraints all play their allotted part and where all the basic assumptions of Buddhism can also be taken for granted. Nor must one forget the Shinto element in the tradition, with its cult of nature on the one hand and its inculcation of the chivalrous virtues on the other; the Japanese soul would not be what it is without both these influences to fashion it. Thus prepared, a man can face both the severity of a Zen training and also that element of the outrageous in Zen which so fascinates minds anxious to react against the conventional values of their own previous background, with its ready-made morality and its conceptual triteness. All these things have to be seen in proportion if they are to be rightly understood.

For those who think that Zen is pure 'self-power' without any 'other power' admixture it is well to point out that at least one of the manifestations of grace listed in this essay plays a most important part there: this is the guru, or roshi who, since he is not the disciple, must needs represent 'other power' in relation to the latter, say what one will. That Zen, despite its constant exhortation to personal effort, does not exclude the *tariki* element was proved to me (if it needed proof) by a Japanese Zen lecturer who came to England some years ago. At the end of his talk I went up to the platform and asked him: 'Is it correct to say that, as between "own power" and "other power", each always will imply the other? If one is affirmed, can one then assume the other as latent, and vice versa?' 'But of course,' the speaker answered. 'They are two sides of the same coin. This is self-evident. Moreover, is not Zen a non-dualistic doctrine?'

A story that has provided many Japanese painters with a subject will further serve to illustrate this same point. This is the story of Zen's redoubtable Patriarch, Bodhidharma, and of his crossing the ocean borne on a reed or sprig of bamboo; for 'ocean', *samsāra* is to be understood, this being the traditional symbolism of the waters all the world over.

It is said that on one occasion Bodhidharma came to the sea-shore wishing to cross to the other side. Finding no boat, he suddenly espied a piece of reed and promptly seized and launched it on the water; then, stepping boldly on its fragile stalk, he let himself be carried to the farther shore. Now, Bodhidharma was a sage; he knew that 'own power' and 'other power', dedicated free will and grace, are in essence the same, and his own use of the reed for a vehicle rests on that very awareness. For us onlookers, however, the point to note is that Bodhidharma *found* that reed on the sea-shore; he neither created it nor brought it with him. Who was it, then, that placed that reed there ready to be discovered? The 'other power'; it could be no other. The reed came to the Zen Patriarch as a grace, to which in the first place he could but be passive; then, having received it, he responded actively by an appropriate initiative and crossed the waters of samsāra to the other shore. Hereby the moral of the Buddha image is pointed once again, if in different form.

By contrast with Zen, the Pure Land doctrine offers itself as a typical way of grace; hence the suggestion put forward by some that *Jodo*, in its early Chinese days, was influenced by Christian teachings brought to China by members of the Nestorian sect from Syria – a gratuitous hypothesis if ever there was one, since *Jōdō* in all essentials remains a typically Buddhist form of wisdom. The following brief outline of the Pure Land teaching will make its theoretical position sufficiently clear for present purposes.

A certain Bodhisattva of the name of Dharmākara was about to enter the state of enlightenment when, moved by compassion, he said to himself: 'How can I bear to enter nirvana when all the multitude of beings have to stay behind, a prey to indefinite transmigration and suffering? Rather than leave them in that state, I vow that if I am not able to deliver them down to the last blade of grass, then let me never reach enlightenment!' But in fact (so the argument runs) he did reach enlightenment and now reigns, as the Buddha Amitabha, over the Western quarter; therefore his vow cannot have failed in its object; suffering beings can and must be delivered, if only they will have faith in Amitabha's vow and call upon his name. This they do through the *nembutsu*, the formula 'Praise to Amitabha Buddha' (in Japanese *Namu Amida Butsu*). Invocation of this formula in selfless reliance on the vow is, for the Pure Land devotee, his constant means of grace, the sign of his unconditional surrender to the 'other power'. To think of effort or merit or knowledge as 'one's own' inevitably implies clinging to a fancied selfhood, disguise this as one will; it violates the first and last condition of deliverance. Who can speak of self-power when he lacks the first idea of what self means?

From here, the Pure Land dialectic goes on to say that in the early days of Buddhism men doubtless were stronger, more self-reliant; they could take severe disciplines and follow ways of meditation of the *jiriki* type. But now, thanks to our bad karma, we are living in the latter days, dark and sin-ridden, when men have grown weak, confused, and above all hopelessly passive. Well, then, says the Pure Land teacher, let this very weakness of theirs be turned to good account; let it offer itself humbly to Amitabha's grace, yielding before the power of his vow. If by the force of his vow the righteous can be delivered, how much more will this be true of sinners whose need is so much greater! Compare with this the words of Christ: 'I came not to call the righteous, but sinners, to repentance'; in their implications the two statements are not so very different.

It is of interest to note that in Tibet a method of invocation exists that is in many ways reminiscent of *nembutsu*. It uses a six-syllable formula of which the mystical associations are too complex to be discussed in a few words; it is enough to know that it is called the *mani mantra* and that its revealer is the Bodhisattva Avalokitēsvara (Chenrezig in Tibetan), who in the heavenly Sangha personifies compassion. For present purposes the significant point to notice is that Chenrezig himself is an emanation of the Western Buddha Amitabha, having taken birth from his head, a mythological feature showing the evident kinship of *mani* and *nembutsu*. A difference worth noting, moreover, is that, whereas

Amitabha's mercy, being that of a Buddha, has a 'static' quality, the compassion of Chenrezig is dynamic, as befits a Bodhisattva who, by definition, operates *in the world* as helper of suffering creatures. Every Bodhisattva as such is in fact a living embodiment of the function of grace.

Before concluding this essay I cannot forbear from pointing out a case of what may be called 'spiritual coincidence', as between two widely separated traditions, the Buddhist and the Islamic; this coincidence is attributable neither to borrowing nor to any cause of a haphazard kind but stems from the very nature of things.

The opening line of the Koran is 'Bismi 'Lāhi 'r-Rahmāni 'r-Rahim', which has usually been translated as 'In the Name of God, the Clement, the Merciful'; in Arabic a common root renders the connection between these two names still closer. Now, some well-instructed Muslim friends have explained to me the difference between the above names consists herein, namely that *Ar-Rahman* refers to God's clemency as an intrinsic quality of the Divine Being, whereas *Ar-Rahim* refers to that quality as projected into the creation. It expresses the dynamic aspect of clemency, mercy poured forth and reaching creatures in the form of grace as well as in other ways. Like the Buddhist compassion, it has a dynamic quality; it must find an object for its exercise. It is easy to see that these two names respectively correspond, in all essentials, to Amitabha and Chenrezig: a shining confirmation from an unexpected quarter!

But let not this surprise us unduly; for in the Pure Land of enlightenment is it not true to say that all religious ways must surely meet?

V

Considerations on the Tantric Alchemy

There are three ways of considering the Tantra, each acceptable in its own degree. First, there is the relatively external way of scholarship, concerned largely with accumulating information and sifting source material. Here questions of influences and origins, and of historical affinities generally, will play a part. Second, there is the essential and normal way of regarding Tantra, which can also be called the traditional way, under its twofold aspect of a wisdom (*prajñā*) and a method (*upāya*) or, in other words, a metaphysical theory (lest we forget it, the primitive meaning of the Greek word *theoria* is 'vision') together with its appropriate means of concentration, its yogic expedients. Third, there is what might be described as a generalised 'tantric sense', whereby it is possible to recognise the existence, in places where the name of Tantra has been unknown, of analogous doctrines and methods, thus providing concurrent evidence in favour of the spiritual methods in question. Let us see how the Tantra will appear when viewed from each of these different angles.

First, the scholarly approach. It should be pointed out from the outset that this manner of regarding the subject (or indeed any subject) can be given both a legitimate and an illegitimate form. The true value of scholarship is an ancillary one; it is obviously advantageous to the student, whether engaged in a strictly religious pursuit or otherwise, to be provided with reliable texts and references of various kinds, a task which he himself, lacking the detailed knowledge and training, could hardly undertake on his own account. Likewise it may be helpful, in an indirect way, to form a picture of the historical background of one's religion; and again, a discussion by experts of the exact bearing of the various technical terms figuring in one's texts can be very useful, since in course of time people often lose sight of certain shades of meaning that these terms will have borne for the authors who first used them and which more or less thoughtless repetition may afterwards have blurred. This applies especially to translated texts. All this pertains to the cardinal Buddhist virtue of 'mindfulness' in varying proportions, from which it can be seen that the conscientious scholar is able to render a genuine, if modest service in this field.

The abusive employment of scholarship, on the other hand, which has become wellnigh all-invading in recent times, consists in examining sacred writings and other religious phenomena in the light, or rather in the darkness, of an inbuilt profane prejudice, with the set purpose of reducing them, one and all, to the status of historical, anthropological or sociological accidents, by an explaining away of every transcendent element to be found there – revelation, inspiration, intellection – in purely humanistic terms. The latest and in many ways deadliest addition to this process of subversion is the psychological interpretation of religion, of which the Freudian and Jungian schools provide two representative forms, the one being avowedly materialistic and hostile, while the other affects a sympathetic attitude on the strength of a deftly nurtured system of equivocations, as between things of a spiritual and of a psychic order; the Tantric doctrines have not escaped an attempted annexation to this point of view and the same applies to Zen. The fact is that until quite recently even Oriental commentators, who might have been expected to see further than their Western colleagues, often exhibited a most uncritical haste in adopting the latest exegetic aberrations and this trend has amounted, in many cases, to a regular intellectual stampede in the face of the modern scientism or, in other words, to an urge towards religious and intellectual suicide. It is necessary to be warned of this danger, which has been spreading far and wide on both sides of the globe until now.

It is under the heading of scholarship, which here must be taken in a very broad sense, that a question is best discussed which has often been raised in connection with the Tantra, namely the relationship (if any) between its Buddhist and Hindu forms. Admittedly, to answer a question like this fully more than conventional scholarship is required; any attempted comment must in fact be accompanied by a certain metaphysical insight, able to look beyond the letter of texts and formulations to the underlying spirit in both the cases under comparison.

When the Tantric writings first began to attract serious notice outside the Indian world, largely thanks to the outstanding studies of a late Chief Justice of the Calcutta High Court, Sir John Woodroffe (better known by his pen-name of Arthur Avalon), the fact that he himself, as a Sanskritist in close touch with Bengali pandits, devoted the greater part of his work to the Hindu *Shaktas* and their doctrines, led to a hasty assumption by many that the Buddhist Tantras, which Arthur Avalon had barely touched on, were but an extension of the Hindu Tantric corpus; existence in both cases of an erotic symbolism, that is to say a representation of reality as the interplay of a pair of conjoint principles respectively pictured as male and female, seemed to lend colour to the above conclusion. It hardly needs saying that this seeming polarisation into two divinities, as Shiva and Shakti in the one case and as the various Buddhas with their female counterparts in the other, implies no radical dualism; despite appearances, the Tantric point of view is non-dualistic through and through, so that it is only at the point of indistinguishable union of the male and female principles thus depicted that the truth is effectively to be found. The male divinity and his partner essentially *are* one another and can never be regarded apart; the static *is* the creative or productive power and vice versa and indeed it is the very fact that a numerical unity has been avoided in the symbolism, in favour of the more subtle idea of non-duality, that makes the Tantric symbolical language so peculiarly eloquent and its corresponding methods so effective in unloosing the hold of dualistic habit on the human mind.[1]

Prior to the publication of Arthur Avalon's series of volumes, the Tantric practices and also their associated iconography had become a favourite target of vicious insinuation, first on the part of ignorant Western commentators, especially missionaries, obsessed with unclean suspicions wherever the word 'sex' was even mentioned and, following their example, also on the part of Westernised Orientals; this prejudice has died hard and it is only in recent decades that the Tantras have begun to be regarded in the world at large as respectable, let alone as spiritually important doctrines. It is largely thanks to observations carried out in the Tibetan field that this welcome if belated change has come about. When one looks back to the end of the last century and the early years of the present one, barring the lonely voice of Avalon, very few foreign writers had a good word to say on the subject. Even as late as 1936 an excellent scholar like the Japanese professor Tajima, himself an adherent of a Tantric school, Shingon, voiced the current prejudice, not against Tantrism as a whole but against the Tibetan forms of it, by suggesting that whereas those Chinese and Japanese Tantric doctrines he himself favoured had originated, historically speaking, from Nalanda, the Tibetan ones, according to him, had mostly issued from Vikramashila, which he wrote off as the home of relatively popular and superstitious beliefs and practices; his evidence for so thinking was, however, by no means clear. In any case, one is minded to ask, What about Naropa and his Six Doctrines, since he certainly belonged to Nalanda? And where would Marpa and Mila Repa and so much of Tibet's finest esoteric flowering have been without these doctrines? If a man as well informed as Professor Tajima could still echo, even faintly, those old prejudices, this but goes to show how thoroughly the various slanderers of Tantra had gone about their work of slinging mud. There is no doubt, however, that it is the denigration of the erotic symbolism that has chiefly helped to fog the issue, over and above whatever genuine problems the question of origins might have presented for better informed minds.

If I may be allowed here to strike a personal note, I should like to explain that when I first became aware of the place of Tantra in Tibetan tradition and art my natural impulse was to fly to its defence, in opposition to the prejudiced reports still current at the time, as described above; in the first flush of discovery that such a thing as a Tantric Buddhism existed and that it was a treasury of beautiful and eminently significant symbols I was ready to give tongue to my enthusiasm, but certainly was not competent to go very far on the interpretative side – Avalon's treatises were then almost my only source of information and very precious they were at the time. That is why I readily resorted to Hindu usage, by referring to the female divinities as 'consort-energies' when writing my first book *Peaks and Lamas*; too much, however, should not be read into this allusion, which was largely accidental and certainly did not amount to a technical appraisal of a definitive kind.

Even at that early date, however, I did perceive one thing, which others have since pointed out from a position of greater information, namely that the sexual symbolism, common to the Buddhist and Hindu Tantra, nevertheless exhibits a divergence between the two schools touching the way in which the sexual attributions are respectively applied; that is to say, in Hindu Tantrism, Shiva (or any other male form of divinity) represents the static aspect while the corresponding female form represents the dynamic or creative aspect; hence her quality of Shakti, female-energy[2], which in Hindu parlance has become the generic term for all heavenly Consorts. In Buddhism, on the other hand, the symbolical pairing takes on an impersonal form (which agrees with the Buddhist spiritual economy in general) and it also works the other way round inasmuch as here it is *prajñā*, the female partner, who seems to indicate the more static aspect of the symbolism – 'wisdom' is essentially a state or quality of being – while the male element in the syzygy is referred to as 'method' (*upāya*), which, on the face of it, carries dynamic implications, since it is thanks to a deploying of the right means, with their accompanying effort, that wisdom is able to be realised in the heart of the devotee. Moreover, the traditional assimilation of *upāya* to *compassion* (itself a dynamic conception) lends additional weight to the view that the Buddhist Tantric symbolism works the opposite way to the Hindu; from which some polemically minded writers, filled with pro-Buddhist patriotism, have gladly drawn the conclusion that Buddhist Tantrism is something entirely alien to the Hindu Tantrism; to which they add as a rider, supported by rather tendentiously selected and interpreted evidence, that it is anterior in origin and that it was the Hindus who borrowed these methods from the Buddhists (as well as other things) and then imposed on them, *a posteriori*, the specifically Hindu notion of power, Shakti.

Without claiming to be a scholar myself, I do not consider an explanation of this kind necessary in order to account for the available evidence and the same applies in regard to criteria of a more profound kind; the truth would rather seem to be that what can, without abuse of language, be called the 'Tantric Revelation' belongs to both the great Indian traditions which it embraced, as it were in answer to a 'cyclic need', in one providential overflowing of the Spirit in a manner that implies no derogation respecting the originality of either traditional form – rather let us see herein an example of that universal and divine Compassion which, in apparent disregard of all rationally delimited frontiers, provides what is needed for the salvation of suffering beings at a given time and place. It is not without reason that the Tantric spiritual methods, wherever these are followed, are regarded as a way most appropriate to the conditions of the present phase of the world cycle, where more primordial and, in a sense, more inflexible ways no longer fully match the need.

To sum up the above view: the representation of non-duality in the guise of a merging of male and female conjugal love, as well as the variously characteristic yogic practices connected therewith, is enough to prove the fundamental kinship between the Hindu and Buddhist Tantra despite some important divergencies as to detail. Granted this basic identity it is going too far, however, to try and establish a point to point correspondence in the respective symbolisms: *shakti* and *prajñā* are not simply interchangeable ideas, and each of the two Tantric currents has evidently given rise to some original features, consonantly with its own peculiar genius, so that the impersonal *prajñā–upāya* relationship that has characterised Mahayana Buddhism on the one hand and the personified presentation characteristic of Hindu theism, *Shiva–Shakti*, on the other, have been able to grow out of the same erotic symbolism without risk of confusion in either direction. I doubt if one will get much nearer the truth of the matter than this.[3]

By way of illustrating what might be described as a 'metaphysical subterfuge', typical in its way, whereby an underlying identity is able to be discerned across an apparent expression of interreligious rivalry, I would like to relate a rather amusing explanation given to me by a lama when I was staying near Shigatse in 1947; we were speaking about the Kailās and its pilgrimage and I had just made the observation that the divinity dwelling on the sacred summit, Demchhog for the Tibetans and Shiva for the Hindus, appeared to have much the same attributes; might one not infer from this, I asked, that Demchhog and Shiva are one and the same divinity and that each is, in effect, the other under a different name? 'You are wrong,' said the lama, 'since Shiva is the name of a Hindu god whom Demchhog challenged in the name of Buddhism and overcame, after which he appropriated his mountain and all his major and minor attributes, his consort included' – a truly delightful way of bypassing traditional differences while seeming to make no concession to the opposite side. Nor must one overlook the fact that, according to this explanation, the lady Pārvatī exchanged her former quality of *Shakti* for that of her new husband's *prajñā* without turning a hair; the long and short of all this being that the situation on Mount Kailās remains unchanged and unchangeable and all ways lead there.

Having dwelt so long on this much-canvassed question of affinities, it will only be possible to touch briefly on the second of our three aspects of Tantra, on what was described at the outset as its normal or traditional aspect. In this connection it may well be asked, in view of the world-wide religious crisis going on today, whether any of the Tantric ways still remain viable for men of the present generation and, if so, what are the conditions allowing a man to opt for this way. The answer is that wherever the traditional structure has withstood the pressure of the times sufficiently to allow a would-be disciple to find a guru qualified to initiate and give instruction there is no reason for him to hold off from following this line; let him profit from any discoverable opportunity while the going is good. If a door that is open today becomes closed tomorrow it will then be time to think again, but there is no reason to anticipate on this worser eventuality. Admittedly, the sacrilegious overrunning of Tibet, the chosen home of Tantra, has left the adjoining countries sadly unsupported; it is as if a bountiful fountain of spiritual influence has suddenly dried up. It would be going too far, however, to say that all opportunities of this kind have disappeared in the neighbouring regions; in Japan also, the Tantric initiations of Shingon and Tendai still carry on, which is marvellous in a country where profane forms of education together with industrialism have been fostered to an extreme degree, as has happened there. It is these developments, fruits of an indiscriminate development of methods minus any corresponding wisdom, which everywhere constitute the greatest threat to religion as well as to life itself. Contemporary man, helpless slave of his own mechanical creations, remains as if suspended between two karmically interconnected explosions, the nuclear one and the 'population explosion'. Lacking all discernment, he diverts to the purveyors of rockets to the moon that admiration which once was offered to the Buddhas and the Saints. This fascination exerted on the human mind by trivialities inflated to monstrous proportions is in fact one of the characteristic notes of the fearful era foretold by Tsong Khapa (and also by the Scriptures of all peoples) when, as he said, 'impure residues grow greater and greater'.

This era is now upon us as part of our karma, which we cannot hope to bypass but have to face. What then is the attitude required of us under these unavoidably distressing circumstances?

Surely the answer every true aspirant will give is this, that 'the world is always the world even when a fair wind is blowing; so also *Bodhi* is *Bodhi* in the foulest weather. Therefore, I myself, be I even left as the sole follower of the Way in a world grown hopelessly inattentive, shall continue to pursue that way and not look back'. There is nothing idealistic about such an attitude; it is prompted by the most practical considerations. The essential message of the Sutras and Tantras does not differ from this.

Though it was natural to refer first, when broaching the above question, to the parent lands of Tantra in Asia, it might also be asked whether, under the exceptional conditions now prevailing, some exporting of Tantric methods might not take place in other directions, leading to a fresh local flowering; those who put this question are usually thinking of the dispersion of Tibetan lamas in various alien lands, whereby some are hoping that a new impetus may be given to slumbering spiritual forces in the West. In fact, during recent years a number of centres have started up in various parts of Europe and America under the direction of Tibetan masters able to confer Tantric initiations and to impart teachings. This has opened fresh doors for many, with unpredictable consequences as regards the future.

It now remains for us to consider what may fittingly be called 'the Spirit of Tantra', our third category in the preamble to this essay. What then are the criteria wherewith to recognise that spirit, wherever it may occur? In its way, this question is important under all circumstances and every man of spiritual intent stands to gain from its answering, even if his own way of realisation does not assume one of the forms coming under the Tantric label. A short discussion of this question will therefore provide a natural conclusion to the present considerations on Tantric spirituality.

Essentially one can speak of a 'Tantric sense' or a 'Tantric spirit' (the former being the faculty wherewith to recognise the presence of the latter) in connection with any doctrine or method of which the conscious aim is a transmutation of the human soul in such a way as to enable the true intelligence, the 'mind of *Bodhi*', to emerge and take command. This process is properly an alchemical one, inasmuch as no element in the soul is actually to be destroyed or cut out; the Tantric technique consists in putting to use whatever exists there, without exception; which in its turn implies the possibility of converting whatever is base or polluted into something pure and noble.

In medieval Europe, as also in the Islamic world, the alchemical sciences were founded on this idea; according to the mineral symbolism they used, lead, the basest metal, was to be transmuted, quickly or by stages, into the solar metal, gold. In the course of this process certain other symbolical substances, notably sulphur and mercury, were called into play at various stages of the alchemical operation. If in the Middle Ages the ignorant sometimes credited the alchemists with a literal intention of getting rich by manufacturing gold from lead, historians of modern science have displayed a similar ignorance in believing that alchemy was simply a primitive attempt to do what the present-day chemist does and that the various materials referred to were what their names indicate and no more; it is thanks to a few investigators who have taken the trouble to study the alchemical writings with proper care and an open mind that this hitherto misunderstood science, so close to the Tantra in intention, has at last been cleared of the crude misconceptions that had gathered round it especially in modern times.[4]

A particularly important point to note, in connection with alchemy, is the recognition, across all apparent differences, of a common essence linking together the two substances to be found at the beginning and end of the transmutative process. If the alchemist in course of his investigations happens to find lead mixed in with other metals, he does not hastily throw it on the scrap-heap since, to his discerning eye, its leaden dullness already masks the potential radiance of pure gold. Therefore he treasures it like the rest while considering the proper means for converting it into what by rights it should be; his attitude is typically non-dualistic and so is his technique. In fact, certain alchemists have declared that lead, or any 'base' metal, is essentially gold fallen sick; gold is lead when free of all trace of illness. One might well parallel this statement, from the Tantric side, by saying that a wordly man is nothing but a sick Buddha; a Buddha is a man who has been wholly healed of his existential sickness.

Together with the idea of transmutation, on which all alchemical processes depend, has gone a certain attitude towards the ethical prescriptions of religion which, in the case of the Tantra, is among those features that have on occasion provoked accusations of moral laxity of the kind alluded to earlier in this essay. This attitude consists in regarding even a person's vices as a source of latent power, as a virtue misapplied but still utilisable if one knows the proper way to handle it; simply to suppress the outward expression of a vicious tendency, by a single-handed effort of the will carried out when in a state of relative unawareness, may not be the most effective way to rid the soul of the tendency in question – not to mention the danger of letting in another and worse evil in order to fill a vacuum created in a psychic substance not yet conditioned to attract a compensating element from a purely spiritual direction. Christ's story of the seven devils rushing in to occupy the house left empty after the expulsion of the single previous devilish occupant provides a vivid illustration of this particular danger. The Tantric or alchemical healer bases certain of his practices on an awareness that, by comparison with the characteristic slipperiness of human thought, a passion often displays a relatively simple and graspable character, such as allows of its being made to serve as the raw material of an alchemical operation in its early stages; to handle a passional element provisionally as a means for an avowedly spiritual purpose does not imply a condoning of passion as such and, still less, any writing down of the virtue whereof that passion is the negative reflexion or shadow. All such a healer does is to view any particular passion in relation to the process of purification considered as a whole, which may sometimes require that it be tolerated provisionally for reasons of psychic equilibrium, though certainly not excused in itself. The true Tantric practitioner is interested in an integral regeneration, nothing less; that is why, for him, every property of body and mind will have its proper place there, the art being to know how to put each thing in its own place, without omission or suppression of any utilisable factor, be appearances as they may. Individual abuses apart, it is in the light of this general principle that those Tantric practices must be judged which have been the occasion of scandal to the conventional moralists; anyone who approaches the question in this way will need no further convincing that the Tantric tradition is as much concerned as exoteric religion with the promotion and practice of the virtues; only its manner of pursuing this purpose goes deeper than symptoms, than the mere form of acts, being in fact most concerned with the medium in which these acts are able to arise, which it tries to transmute so that only virtue is able to survive there.

A virtue, for one engaged on any esoteric path, is primarily a mode of knowing or, to be more accurate, a factor dispositive to enlightenment. Similarly, a vice will be rated as a factor of ignorance, or as a cause of thickening the existential veil between the human subject and the light; this way of regarding good and evil is a properly intellectual one, the usual perspective of merit and demerit being, by comparison, relatively external and dualistic, but not wholly untrue for that – indeed far from it. To practise a virtue is then like clearing a window in the soul; to indulge in a vice is like smearing that same window with dirt. That is why the practice of the virtues is not less important for one pursuing the way of knowledge than for the man of action or the man of loving piety (for the latter it is pleasing or offending the Beloved that counts); more or less enigmatic references in the Tantric writings to the man for whom the distinction between good and evil has ceased to matter need not deceive anyone on that score.

No better description of Tantra, in a European language, can be found than to call it an 'alchemical science of the soul' whereby the lead of samsaric existence becomes transmuted into what it already is in principle, namely the Bodhic gold, eternally gleaming.

NOTES

1 The Chinese symbolism of *yin-yang* conveys a similar message: here *yin*, the female principle portrayed as dark in hue and representing the passive and potential side of things (*Shakti* might well be rendered as 'potency') and *yang*, the male, light of hue and representing their active or essential side, are combined in a circular diagram (in its way a kind of mandala), the interlocked halves of which evidently correspond to a marriage between them; each half moreover displays one tiny spot of the opposing colour whereby is indicated the non-dualistic interpenetration of the principles thus depicted.

2 It might be mentioned, in passing, as an instructive example of spiritual coincidence, that in the Christian Church under its Orthodox (Eastern) form the doctrine of the 'Divine Energies', first fully expounded by the great fourteenth-century doctor St Gregory Palamas, is distinctly reminiscent of the Hindu idea of Shakti which the word 'energy' admirably

renders. According to the Palamite theology God creates the world not by His Essence but by His Energies.

3 Similar views have been expressed by the late Dr S. B. Dasgupta in his abundantly documented *Introduction to Tantric Buddhism* published by the University of Calcutta in 1950; second edition 1958. This distinguished scholar, while paying just tribute to the extent and variety of the Buddhist Tantric literature, nevertheless maintains and, as it seems to me, substantiates the thesis that Tantricism, whether Hindu or Buddhistic, remains fundamentally the same. He certainly does not overlook any of the differences of expression and practice that distinguish the two traditions. His appraisal of the basic theology behind the symbolism is clear and concise, while the wealth of illustration and commentary is of the most satisfying proportions. It is noteworthy that here and there in this book the author refers to one or other Buddhist goddess as the *shakti* of her corresponding male divinity: the content shows, in every case, that here he is making a purely conventional use of the term as is but natural in one Indian-born; had he been speaking of the Hellenic gods, he would doubtless have referred to Hera as the *shakti* of Zeus: nothing further is to be read into this proceeding on his part, which explains itself at a glance. All that one can usefully add is to say that, given the slight verbal inaccuracy of introducing the term *shakti* into a Buddhist context, the word 'Consort' (which adequately renders the Tibetan *Yum*) is to be preferred as precluding all possible terminological confusions.

4 One of the best documented, as well as intelligible, works on the subject now available is *Alchemy*, by Titus Burckhardt, published by Penguin Books, Baltimore, USA.

VI

Nembutsu as Remembrance[1]

Were one to put the question wherein consist the differences between Theravada, the Buddhism of the Pali Canon, and the Mahayana with its vast variety of schools and methods, one might for a start mention the particular emphasis laid, in the Mahayana teachings, upon the cosmic function of the Bodhisattva: saying this does not mean that in relation to the Theravada the Bodhisattvic ideal constitutes some kind of innovation; it suffices to read the Jātakas or stories about the Buddha Sakyamuni's previous births in order to find those characteristic postures which the word 'Bodhisattva' came to imply in subsequent centuries here prefigured in mythological mode.[2] These stories were current long before the distinction between Theravada and Mahayana came in vogue; since then they have remained as common means of popular instruction extending to every corner of the Buddhist world. Nevertheless it is fair to say that, with the Mahayana, the Bodhisattva as a type steps right into the centre of the world-picture, so much so that 'the Bodhisattva's Vow' to devote himself consciously to the salvation of all beings without exception might well be considered as marking a man's entry into the Mahayana as such; viewed in this light, whatever occurs at a time prior to his taking this decisive step must be accounted an aspiration only, one waiting to be given its formal expression through the pronouncing of the vow, when the hour for this shall have struck.

By its root meaning the word 'Bodhisattva' denotes one who displays an unmistakable affinity for enlightenment, one who tends in that direction both deliberately and instinctively. In the context of the Buddhist path it indicates one who has reached an advanced stage;[3] such a man is the dedicated follower of the Buddha in principle and in fact. If all this is commonly known, what we are particularly concerned with here, however, is to extract from the Bodhisattvic vocation its most characteristic trait, as expressed in the words of the Vow which run as follows: 'I, so and so, in the presence of my Master, so and so, in the presence of the Buddhas, do call forth the idea of Enlightenment. . . . I adopt all creatures as mother, father, brothers, sons, sisters, and kinsmen. Henceforth . . . for the benefit of creatures I shall practise charity, discipline, patience, energy, meditation, wisdom[4] and the means of application . . . let my Master accept me as a future Buddha.'

It can be seen at a glance that this profession of intent anticipates, by implication, the vow taken by the Bodhisattva Dharmakara from which the Pure Land teaching and practice stem. He who first had vowed to dedicate himself wholeheartedly to the good of his fellow creatures, 'down to the last blade of grass' as the saying goes, after treading the Path from life to life or else, in an exceptional case like that of Tibet's poet-saint Milā Repa, in the course of a single life, finds himself clearly set for the great awakening; his unremitting efforts, canalised thanks to the proper *upāyas* (means) matching each successive need, have placed him in possession of *prajnā*, that wisdom whereby all things in a formerly opaque world have been rendered transparent to the light of Bodhi – it is at this crucial point that the Bodhisattva renews his vow to succour all beings. This time, however, he gives to his vow a negative as well as a more intensive turn by saying that 'I shall *not* enter nirvana unless I be assured that I can draw after me all the other creatures now steeped in ignorance and consequent suffering': through this vow the Bodhisattva's compassion becomes endowed with irresistible force; aeons of well-doing pass as in a flash; countless creatures are lifted out of their misery, until one day the cup of Dharmakara's merit overflows, and lo! we find ourselves face to face with Amitabha radiating in all directions his saving light. By this token we are given to understand that the vow has not failed in its object; the Buddha himself stands before us offering tangible proof of the vow's efficacy through the communication of his Name under cover of the *nembutsu*; henceforth this will suffice to ferry across the troubled waters of samsāra any being who will confidently trust his sin-weighted body to this single vehicle, even as Zen's stern patriarch Bodhidharma once trusted the reed he picked up on the water's edge and was borne safely upon its slender stalk across to the other shore. Such is the story of the providential birth of Jodo-shin.

Reduced to bare essentials *nembutsu* is first of all an act of remembrance, whence attention follows naturally[5] thus giving rise to faith in, and thankfulness for, the Vow. From these elementary attitudes a whole programme of life can be deduced.

Given these properties comprised by the *nembutsu* as providential reminder and catalyst of the essential knowledge, it should cause no one any surprise to hear that comparable examples of the linking of a divine Name with an invocatory *upāya* are to be found elsewhere than in China and Japan; details will of course be different, but the same operative principle holds good nevertheless. To point this out is in no wise to impugn the spiritual originality of the message delivered by the agency of the two great patriarchs, Honen and Shinran Shonin, within the framework of Japanese Buddhism with effects lasting even to this day; on the contrary, this is but further proof of the universal applicability of this method to the needs of mankind, and more especially during a phase of the world-cycle when the hold of religion on human minds seems to be weakening in the face of a vast and still growing apparatus of distraction such as history has never recorded before. The fact that the obvious accessibility of such a method does not exclude the most profound insights – indeed the contrary is true – has turned *nembutsu* and kindred methods to be found elsewhere into potent instruments of regeneration even under the most unfavourable circumstances: this gives the measure of their timeliness as well as of their intrinsic importance.

As an example of mutual corroboration between traditions, I have chosen a form of invocation current in the Tibetan-cum-Mongolian world where however, it is not, as in Japan, associated with any particular school but is in fact widely used by adherents of all schools without distinction. Other examples might also have been chosen belonging to non-Buddhist traditions, but it has seemed best to confine one's choice to places nearer home both because one can continue to use a common terminology and also, more especially, because in the Tibetan version the Buddha

Amitabha figures in a manner which makes this tradition's kinship with Jodo-shin clearly apparent.

The operative formula in this case is the six-syllable phrase *Om mani padme Hum* of which the acknowledged revealer is the Bodhisattva Chenrezig (*Avalokitesvara* in Sanskrit, *Kwannon* in Japanese). It is his intimate relationship with the Buddha Amitabha which provides the mythological link between the two traditions in question. In order to illustrate this point it will be necessary to hark back to the moment when the Bodhisattva Dharmakara became transfigured into the Buddha of Infinite Light; what we shall have to say now will be something of a sequel to the history of Dharmakara's ascent to Buddhahood as previously related.

If one stops to examine that history somewhat more closely one will become aware of a fact replete with meaning, namely that it would be possible without the least inconsistency to reverse the emphasis by saying that it is an Amitabha about to be who has been replaced by a Dharmakara fulfilled. In other words, if Buddhahood as such represents a state of awareness or knowledge, Bodhisattva-hood when fully realised, as in this case, represents the dynamic dimension of that same awareness; *it is* that awareness in dynamic mode. It is moreover evident that this latter mode of awareness can only be realised in relation to an object in view; if the rescue of suffering beings be its ostensible motive, then this dynamic quality will necessarily take on the character of *compassion*, the Bodhisattvic virtue already specified in the elementary version of the vow; such a virtue moreover postulates a given world for its exercise, apart from which compassion would not even be a possible concept.

As the dynamic expression of *that* which Buddhahood is statically, Bodhisattvahood belongs to this world; it is with perfect logic that the Mahayana teachings have traditionally identified compassion with 'method'. Method is the dynamic counterpart of 'wisdom', the quality of awareness: try to separate these two ideas and they will forfeit all practical applicability, hence the Mahayana dictum that Wisdom and Method form an eternal syzygy excluding any possibility of divorce. The Bodhisattva incarnates method as exercisable in samsāra; the Buddha personifies wisdom as ever-present in nirvana: this leaves us with two complementary triads, namely 'Bodhisattva – this world – method' and 'Buddha – Buddha-field (=Pure Land) – wisdom'. 'Human life hard of obtaining' is the opportunity to realise these complementary possibilities; if the saying be true that at the heart of each grain of sand a Buddha is to be found, it is no less true to say that in every being a potential Bodhisattva is recognisable, in active mode in the case of a man, in relatively passive mode in the case of other beings but nonetheless realisable by them via the prior attainment of a human birth.[6]

From all the above it follows that a Bodhisattva's activity on behalf of beings does not lose its necessity once Buddhahood is attained; the ascending course from Dharmakara to Amitabha, as confirmed by the Vow, must needs have its counterpart in a descending course under a fresh name. This name in fact is Chenrezig or Kwannon who, as the story tells us, took birth from the head of Amitabha himself, thus becoming the appointed dispenser of a mercy which is none other than a function of the nirvanic Light; in Chenrezig we see a Dharmakara as it were nirvanically reborn, if such an expression be permissible. Here again the story of this celestial event is illuminating, since we are told that Chenrezig, in his exercise of the merciful task laid upon him by his originator and teacher Amitabha, began by leading so many beings towards the promised Buddha-land that the very hells became emptied. However, when this Bodhisattva looked back upon the world, just as his predecessor Dharmakara had done prior to taking his vow, he perceived the horrifying fact that as quickly as one lot of beings climbed out of the infernal round of birth and death following in his wake, another lot of beings, in apparent unconcern, hastened to fill the vacant places, so that the mass of samsaric suffering remained virtually as bad as ever. The Bodhisattva was so overcome by disappointment and pity that his head split in fragments, whereupon the Buddha came to the rescue with a fresh head for his representative. This same thing happened no less than ten times until, with the bestowing by Amitabha of an eleventh head, the Bodhisattva was enabled to resume his mission without further hindrance.

In the Tibetan iconography Chenrezig is frequently portrayed under his eleven-headed form, appropriately known as the 'Great Compassionate One'; multiple arms go with this portrait, as showing the endless ways in which the Bodhisattva can exercise his function as helper of beings. The most usual portrait of Chenrezig, however, is one with four arms, the whole figure being coloured white; in one hand he holds a rosary and it is this object which symbolises his communication of the *mani* as invocatory means.

Some details of how the invocation with *mani* is carried out by the Tibetans will serve to relate the practice to other similar methods found in Japan and elsewhere.

First, about the formula itself: the most usual translation into English has been 'Om, jewel in the Lotus, Hum'. Obviously, such words do not immediately lend themselves to logical paraphrase; one can reasonably assume, however, that since in the traditional iconography Buddhas are normally shown as seated upon a lotus, that serene flower resting on the waters of possibility and thereby evocative of the nature of things, the jewel must for its part represent the presence of the Buddha and the treasure of his teaching inviting discovery, but this by itself does not get one very far. As for the initial and concluding syllables, these belong to the category of metaphysically potent ejaculations whereof many figure in the Tantric initiations: one can safely say, with this kind of formula, that it is not intended for analytical dissection, but rather that its intrinsic message will spontaneously dawn upon a mind poised in one-pointed concentration. This view, moreover, was confirmed by the Dalai Lama when I put to him the question of whether the *mani* would by itself suffice to take a man all the way to Deliverance. His Holiness replied that it would indeed suffice for one who had penetrated to the heart of its meaning, a ruling which itself bears out the saying that the *Om mani padme Hum* contains 'the quintessence of the teaching of all the Buddhas'. The fact that the Dalai Lama specifically exercises an 'activity of presence' in this world in the name of the Bodhisattva Chenrezig, revealer of *mani*, renders his comment in this instance all the more authoritative.

As in all similar cases an initiatory *lung* (authorisation) must be sought by whoever wishes to invoke with *mani*, failing which the practice would remain irregular and correspondingly inefficacious. Once the *lung* has been conferred it is possible to invoke in a number of ways, either under one's breath or, more often, in an audible murmur for which the Tibetan word is the same as for the purring of a cat. It is recommended, for one invoking regularly, that he precede each invoking session by a special poem of four lines and likewise repeat a similar quatrain by way of conclusion. Here is the text:

I

Unstained by sin and white of hue
Born from the head of the perfect Buddha
Look down in mercy upon beings
To Chenrezig let worship be offered.

II

By the merit of this [invocation] may I soon
Become endowed with Chenrezig's power.
Let all beings without even one omission
In his [Chenrezig's] land established be.

No need to underline the reference to Amitabha in the first verse
and the reference to the Buddha-land in the second in order to
show how close to one another *mani* and *nembutsu* stand as regards
their basic purpose.

Mention should also be made here of the standard treatise on
the *mani* invocation, in which are outlined the various symbolical
correspondences to which the six syllables lend themselves, each
of which can become a theme for meditation. These sixfold schemes
range over a wide field, starting with deliverance from each in
turn of the possible states of sentient existence and the realisation
one by one of the six *pāramitās* or Transcendent Virtues (see again
note 4 on page 100); the latter parts of this treatise lead the mind
into still deeper waters which it is beyond the scope of this essay
to explore.

To turn to more external features of the *mani* invocation, it is
common practice to use some kind of rhythmical support while
repeating the words of the mantra, which can be either a rosary or
else an appliance peculiar to Tibet which foreign travellers have
rather inappropriately (since no idea of petition enters in) labelled as
a 'prayer-wheel'. This wheel consists of a rotating box fixed on the
end of a wooden handle and containing a tightly rolled cylinder of
paper inscribed all over with the *mani* formula. A small weight
attached by a chain to the box enables the invoking person to
maintain an even swing while repeating the words; sometimes,
especially with elderly people, the practice becomes reduced to a
silent rotatory motion, with the invocation itself taken for granted.

Very large *mani*-wheels are commonly to be found at the doors
of temples, so that people as they enter may set them in motion;
likewise, rows of smaller wheels are often disposed along the

outside walls so that those who carry out the *pradakshinam* or clockwise circuit of the sacred edifice may set them revolving as they pass. But remembrance of the *mani* does not stop there; immense *mani*-wheels ceaselessly kept going by waterfalls exist in many places, while flags bearing the sacred words float from the corners of every homestead. Lastly, flat stones carved with the formula and dedicated as offerings by the pious are to be found laid in rows on raised parapets at the edge of highroads or along the approaches to monasteries. These '*mani*-walls' are so disposed as to allow a passage on either side, since reverence requires that a man turn his right side towards any sacred object he happens to pass, be it a *stupa* or one of these *mani*-walls; being on horseback is no excuse for doing otherwise. The popular dictum 'beware of the devils on the left-hand side' refers to this practice.

If it be asked what effect all this can amount to, the answer is that it serves to keep people constantly reminded of what a human life is for; reminiscence is the key to a religiously directed life at all levels, from the most external and popular to the most interior and intellectual; 'popular' may often be allied with deep insights, of course, for the above distinctions are not intended in a social sense. Certainly in the Tibet we visited while the traditional order there was still intact the whole landscape was as if suffused by the message of the Buddha's Dharma; it came to one with the air one breathed, birds seemed to sing of it, mountain streams hummed its refrain as they bubbled across the stones, a dharmic perfume seemed to rise from every flower, at once a reminder and a pointer to what still needed doing. The absence of fear on the part of wild creatures at the approach of man was in itself a witness to this same truth; there were times when a man might have been forgiven for supposing himself already present in the Pure Land. The India of King Ashoka's time must have been something like this; to find it in mid-twentieth-century anywhere was something of a wonder.

Moreover a situation like this was bound to be reflected in the lives of individuals, despite inevitable human failings; piety was refreshingly spontaneous, it did not need dramatising attitudes to bolster it up nor any rationalised justifications. Each man was enabled to find his own level without difficulty according to capacity and even a quite modest qualification could carry him far. Among the many people using the *mani* one can say that a large proportion stopped short at the idea of gathering merit with a view to a favourable rebirth; the finality in view, though not entirely negligible in itself, remained essentially samsaric: it did not look far beyond the limits of the cosmos. More perceptive practitioners would resort to the same invocation for the general purpose of nourishing and deepening their own piety; the finality here was 'devotional', in the sense of the Indian word *bhakti*, implying a comparatively intense degree of participation; such a way of invoking represents an intermediate position in the scale of spiritual values. Rarer by comparison is the kind of person whose intelligence, matured in the course of the practice, is able to envisage that truth for which the invocation provides both a means of recollection and an incentive to realise it fully; this is the case to which the Dalai Lama was referring when he spoke of penetrating to the heart of the teaching which the Six Syllables between them enshrine.

In a more general connection, the question often arises as to how much importance should be attached to the frequent repetition of a formula like the *mani* or the *nembutsu* compared with a sparser use of it; here one can recall the fact that in the period when Honen was preaching the Pure Land doctrine in Japan many persons, carried away by their enthusiasm, vied with one another as to the number of times they were able to repeat the formula, as if this were the thing that mattered. In the face of such extravagances Shinran Shonin applied a wholesome corrective by showing that the value of *nembutsu* is primarily a qualitative one, with number counting for nothing in itself as a criterion of effectiveness. The essence of a thing, that which makes it to be what it is and not something else, is not susceptible of multiplication: one can for instance count one, two or a hundred sheep, but the quality of 'sheepness' becomes neither increased nor subdivided thereby. The same applies to *nembutsu* or *mani*; each represents a unique and total presence carrying within itself its own finality irrespective of number, situation or timing. This is an important principle to grasp; were one able to penetrate as far as the very heart of the sacred formula a single mention of it would be sufficient to bring one home to the Pure Land; the various steps that have led one as far as the threshold become merged in fulfilment.

At the same time, on the basis of an empirical judgement, one is not justified in despising the man who finds frequent repetition of an invocatory formula helpful; to estimate the value of such repetition in purely quantitative terms is certainly an error, but to feel an urge to fill one's life with the formula because one values it above everything else and feels lonely and lost without it is another thing. To rise of a morning with *nembutsu*, to retire to bed at night with its words on one's lips, to live with it and by it, to die with its last echo in one's ear, what could in fact be better or more humanly appropriate? Between one who invokes very often and another who does so with less frequency there is little to choose provided attention is focused on the essential. It is the effects on the soul which will count in the long run, its alchemical transmutation in witness of the Vow's power, thanks to which the lead of our existential ignorance is enabled to reveal its essential identity with the Bodhic gold, even as Dharmakara's identity with Amitabha is revealed in the Vow itself.

There is one more question of practical importance for all who would follow a contemplative discipline outside the monastic order which here does not concern us, namely the question of how one may regard the interruptions imposed by the need to transfer attention, during one's working hours, to external matters either of a professional kind or else, in the majority of cases, as means of earning a livelihood. Does not this, some may well ask, render the idea of a lifelong concentration on *nembutsu* virtually unrealisable? And, if so, what result will this have in regard to the essential awakening of faith? Some such question has in fact always worried mankind in one form or another, but has become more pressing than ever as a result of the breakdown of traditional societies formerly structured according to religiously linked vocations. The individual is now left in so-called freedom to make choices which his ancestors were mercifully spared. Nevertheless, there is sufficient precedent to enable one to answer this question in a way that all may understand.

The criterion which applies in such cases is this, namely that so long as a man's work is not obviously dishonest, cruel or otherwise reprehensible, that is to say as long as it conforms, broadly speaking,[7] to the definitions of the Noble Eightfold Path under the headings of Proper Ordering of Work and Proper Livelihood, the time and attention this demands from a man will not *per se* constitute a distraction in the technical sense of the word; rather will the stream of contemplation continue to flow quietly like an underground river, ready to surface again with more animated current once the necessary tasks have been accomplished for the time being. Here 'necessary' is the operative word: activities undertaken needlessly, from frivolous or luxurious motives such as a wish to kill time because one expects to feel bored when not actually working, cannot on any showing be ranked as work in the proper sense. A vast number of so-called 'leisure activities' fall under this condemnable heading: these do, on any logical showing, constitute distractions in the strict sense of the word. One would have thought that the briefest portion of a 'human life hard of obtaining' could have been put to better uses; yet nowadays such abuse of the human privilege is not only tolerated but even encouraged on the vastest scale by way of tribute to the great god of Economics, Mara's fashionable alias in the contemporary world. By rights most of these time-wasting practices belong to the category of noxious drugs, addiction to which comes only too easily.

Apart from this question of man's occupational calls and how these properly fit in, the invocation with *nembutsu* or its equivalents in other traditions will always offer a most potent protection against distractions of whatever kind. A life filled with this numinous influence leaves little chance for Mara's attendant demons to gain a footing. I remember one lama's advice when he said, 'Finish the work in hand and after that fill the remaining time with *mani* invocation.' This sets the pattern of a life's programme, details of which can be left to settle themselves in the light of particular needs.

The heart-moving tale of Dharmakara's journey to enlightenment, on which our own participation in the teachings of Jodo-shin depends, may at first sight appear to record events dating from long, long ago. It is well to remember, however, what has already been said (see note 2 on page 99) about the timeless nature of mythological happenings, whereby they are rendered applicable again and again, across the changing circumstances of mankind, as means of human illumination. There are certain truths which are best able to communicate themselves in this form without any danger of entanglement in the alternative of belief versus disbelief which, in the case of historical claims, is all too likely to be raised by the very nature of the evidence on which those claims rest: question the factual evidence, and the truths themselves become vulnerable, as has been shown in the case of Western Christianity during recent times where the attempt to 'demythologise' its sacred lore, including the Scriptures, has only made the situation worse for present-day believers. Historical evidence of course has its own importance – no need to deny this fact. In relation to history a traditional mythology provides a factor of equilibrium not easily dispensed with if a given religion is to retain its hold over the minds of men.

As it stands, the old story of Dharmakara represents the Wisdom aspect of a teaching whereof the Method aspect is to be found when this same story comes to be reenacted in a human life, be it our own life or another's, thanks to the evocative power released by the original Vow, following its confirmation in the person of Amitabha Buddha. Hence the injunction to place all our faith in the Other Power, eschewing self. The consequences of so doing will affect both our thinking and feeling and all we do or avoid doing in this life.

Here it is well to remind ourselves of what was said at the outset, namely that the Bodhisattva's compassion, his dynamic virtue, needs a field for its exercise as well as suffering beings for its objects, failing which it would be meaningless. For a field one can also say 'a world' either in the sense of a particular world (the world familiar to us, for example) or in the sense of samsāra as such, comprising all possible forms of existence, including many we can never know. A world, by definition, is a field of contrasts, an orchard of karma replete with its fruits, black or white, which we ourselves, in our dual capacity of creators and partakers of these fruits, are called upon to harvest in season, be they bitter or sweet. This experiencing of the world, moreover, also comes to us in a dual way, at once external and internal: for us, the external world is composed of all beings and things which fall into the category of 'other', while to the internal world there belong all such experiences as concern what we call 'I' or 'mine', the ego-consciousness at every level. One can go further and say that man, in this respect, himself constitutes something like a self-contained world; it is not for nothing that the human state has been described, by analogy with the Cosmos at large, as a 'microcosm', a little world. It is in fact within this little estate of ours that the drama of Dharmakara and Amitabha has to be played out if we are truly to understand it, this being in fact the Method aspect of the story which thus, through its concrete experiencing, will reveal itself as Wisdom to our intelligence. It is with this, for us, most vital matter that the present essay may fittingly be concluded.

The three principal factors in our symbolical play are, first, the psycho-physical vehicle of our earthly existence which provides the moving stage and, second, the faculty of attention under its various aspects including the senses, reason, imagination, and above all our active remembrance or mindfulness. These between them represent the Bodhisattvic dynamism in relation to our vocational history; third and last, there is the illuminative power of Amitabha as represented by the unembodied Intelligence dwelling at that secret spot in the centre of each being where samsāra as such as inoperative[8] or, to put the point still more precisely, where samsāra reveals its own essential identity with nirvana; but for this Bodhic Eye enshrined within us, able to read the Bodhic message all things display to him who knows where to look, human liberation through enlightenment, and the liberation from suffering of other beings via a human birth, would not be a possibility; the door to the Pure Land would remain for ever closed. Thanks to Dharmakara's example, culminating in his Vow, we know that this Pure Land is open, however; herein consists our hope and our incentive. What more can one ask of existence than this supreme opportunity the human state comprises so long as that state prevails?

Before quitting this discussion one other question calls for passing consideration, affecting the manner of presenting Jodo-shin ideas in popular form today. Writers on the subject seem much given to stressing the 'easy' nature of the Jodo-shin way; faith, so they say, is all we really need inasmuch as Amitabha, Dharmakara that was, has done our work for us already, thus rendering entry into the Pure Land as good as assured, with the corollary that any suggestion of responsibility or conscious effort on our part would savour of a dangerous concession to Own Power and is in any case redundant. In voicing such ideas a sentimentally angled vocabulary is used without apparently taking into account the effect this is likely to have on uncritical minds. Though this kind of language is doubtless not actually intended to minimise the normal teachings of Buddhism, it does nevertheless betray a pathetically artless trend in the thinking of authors who resort to it. Some will doubtless seek to defend themselves by saying that the writings of Shinran and other Jodo-shin luminaries also contain phrases having a somewhat similar ring; those who quote thus out of context are apt to ignore the fact that a teaching sage, one who is out to win hearts but not to destroy intelligences (this should not need saying), may sometimes resort to a schematic phraseology never meant to be taken literally. Lesser persons should show prudence in how they quote from, and especially in how they themselves embroider upon, such statements of the great.

When, for example, Nichiren, that militant saint, declared that a single pronouncing of the *nembutsu* was enough to send a man to hell, he was obviously exaggerating for the purpose of goading his own audience in a predetermined direction; religious history offers many such examples of rhetorical excess, albeit spiritually motivated. The proper reply to such a diatribe would be to say, in the tone of respect due to a great Master, 'Thanks Reverend Sir, your warning brings great comfort; for me Hell with *nembutsu* will be as good as Heaven; without *nembutsu* paradise would be a hell indeed!'[9]

Let us, however, for a moment, as an *upāya* nicely matched to the occasion, carry the argument of the very people we had been criticising a little further by putting the following question: if Dharmakara's compassionate initiative, culminating in the Vow, has come to the aid of our weakness by completing the most essential part of our task for us, leaving it to us to take subsequent advantage of this favour, how best can we repay our debt of gratitude for the mercy shown us? Surely an elementary gratitude requires, on the part of a beneficiary, that he should try and please his benefactor by doing as he has advised and not the contrary. The Eightfold Path is what the Buddha left for our life's programme; in following this way, whether we are motivated by regard for our own highest interest or by simple thankfulness for Amitabha's mercy makes little odds in practice, though this second attitude may commend itself to our mentality for contingent reasons. To bring all this into proper perspective in the context of Jodo-shin one has to bear in mind its operative principle, namely that the *nembutsu* itself comprises all possible teachings, all methods, all merits 'eminently', requiring nothing else of us except our faith, which must be freely given. A genuine faith, however one may regard it, does not go without its heroic overtones; how then are we to understand it in relation to the finality of Jodo-shin, as symbolised by the Pure Land? Surely, in this same perspective, faith is there to act as catalyst of all the other virtues, whether we list them separately or not. In this way an attitude that may sometimes seem one-sidedly devotional can still rejoin Buddhism's profoundest insights; for one who does so, the way may well be described as 'easy'.

What is certain, however, is that no Buddhist, whatever his own personal affiliations may happen to be, can reasonably claim exclusive authority for the teachings he follows; as between an 'Own Power' and an 'Other Power' approach to salvation we can perhaps say that if the latter may sometimes take on a too passive appearance as in the cases previously mentioned, the former type of method, if improperly conceived, can easily imprison one in a state of self-centred consciousness of a most cramping kind. The best defence against either of the above errors is to remember that, between two indubitably orthodox but formally contrasted teachings, where one of them is deliberately stressed the other must always be recognised as latent, and vice versa. This excludes moreover any temptation to indulge in sectarian excesses. No spiritual method can be totally self-contained; by definition every *upāya* is provisionally deployed in view of the known needs of a given mentality; there its authority stops: to say so of any particular teachings implies no disrespect.

The stress laid on 'Other Power' in Jodo-shin provides a salutary counterblast to any form of self-esteem, a fact which makes its teachings peculiarly apt in our own time when deification of the human animal as confined to this world and a wholesale pandering to his ever-expanding appetites is being preached on every side. In the presence of Amitabha the achievements of individual mankind become reduced to their proper unimportance; it is in intelligent humility that a truly human greatness is to be found.

One important thing to bear in mind, in all this, is that the Buddha's mercy is providential, but does not, for this very reason, suspend the Law of Karma: if beings will persist in ignoring that law while coveting the things mercy might have granted them, that mercy itself will reach them in the guise of severity; severity is merciful when this is the only means of provoking a radical *metanoia* (change of outlook), failing which wandering in samsāra must needs continue indefinitely. The *nembutsu* is our ever-present reminder of this truth; if, in reliance on the Vow, we abandon all wish to attribute victory to ourselves, the unfed ego will surely waste away, leaving us in peace.

Apart from all else, reliance on 'Other Power' will remain unrealisable so long as the egocentric consciousness is being mistaken for the real person; it is this confusion of identity which the great *upāya* propounded by Honen and Shinran Shonin was providentially designed to dispel. Let *nembutsu* serve as our perpetual defence against this fatal error, through the remembrance it keeps alive in human hearts. Where that remembrance has been raised to its highest power, there is to be found the Pure Land.

NOTES

1 The word *nembutsu* is a compressed form of the phrase *namu amida butsu*, itself a Japanese reduction of the Sanskrit formula *namo'mitābhaya buddhaya*. The literal meaning is 'praise to Amitabha Buddha'; here *namo* must be taken as comprising the faith, veneration and gratitude which suffering beings owe to the Buddha as dispenser of light; the name 'Amitabha' itself means 'infinite light'. This formula has provided its invocatory *mantram* for the Pure Land school of Buddhism; this 'buddha-field' is named after Amitabha's paradise, symbolically situated in the West. The Pure Land teachings, first enunciated by the Indian masters Nagarjuna and Vasubhandu, reached Japan via China and became widely diffused thanks to the example of two great saints, Honen (1133–1212) and his preeminent disciple Shinran (1173–1262), who gave its present form to the tradition under the name of *Jodo-Shinshu* (=Pure Land true sect): with us, 'sect' has an unhappy sound, but it has become conventional to use it in this context without any opprobrious implications. These elementary facts should be sufficient to prepare readers unacquainted with Japanese Buddhism for what is to follow.

2 The epithet 'mythological' has been introduced here advisedly, in order to draw attention to an important feature of traditional communication which modern terminological usage has tended to debase. The Greek word *mythos*, from which our word derives, originally just meant a story and not a particular kind of story, supposedly fictitious, as nowadays. It was taken for granted that such a story was a carrier of truth, if only because, for the unsophisticated mentality of people brought up on the great myths, anything different would have seemed pointless; the idea of a fictional literature intended as a passing means of entertainment was quite alien to that mentality, and so was allegory of a contrived kind, however elevated its purpose. As a factor in human intelligence a 'mythological sense' corresponds to a whole dimension of reality which, failing that sense, would remain inaccessible. Essentially, myths belong to no particular

time; there is an ever-present urgency about the events they relate which is the secret of their power to influence the souls of mankind century after century.

3 In Tibet the word for Bodhisattva, side by side with its more technical uses, is often loosely applied where, in English, we would use the word 'saintly'; this is not surprising really, since a saintly person evidently exhibits traits appropriate to an incipient Bodhisattvahood.

4 The six *pāramitās* or Transcendent Virtues: according to Mahayana convention *dāna*, the readiness to give oneself up to the service of others, charity in the broadest sense, heads the list as being the 'note' whereby a Bodhisattva can be recognised. It is, however, unlikely that a man would have reached such a pitch of self-abnegation without previously espousing a religiously inspired life of discipline, *shīla*, under its double heading of conscious abstention from sin and positive conformity with the ritual, doctrinal and other prescriptions of the religion in question; such conformity does not go without effort, *vīrya*, the combative spirit. As complement to the above outgoing virtues, *shanti*, contentment, repose in one's own being, follows naturally. It is after a certain blending of these three virtues that the urge into *dāna* may be expected to be felt strongly, thus pointing the way to a Bodhisattva's vocation. The last two *pāramitās*, namely *dhyāna*, contemplation, itself implying discernment between what is real and what is illusory, and *prajnā*, that transcendent wisdom which is a synthesis of all other virtues, completes their scheme of life for followers of the Mahayana: obviously this general pattern is applicable in other religions besides Buddhism.

5 In the Islamic world the word *dhikr*, remembrance, is used of the invocation practised by members of the Sufi confraternities with the Divine Name as its operative formula; the Buddhist term *smrti* and the Sufic *dhikr* bear an identical meaning.

6 For an unusually illuminating commentary on the relationship Bodhisattva – Buddha the reader is referred to Part III of *In the Tracks of Buddhism* by Frithjof Schuon, published by Allen & Unwin, a work to which the present writer gratefully acknowledges his own indebtedness.

7 'Broadly speaking': this reservation was necessary, inasmuch as no person is in a position to assess all the repercussions of his work or his livelihood in an ever-changing world. All he can do is to avoid practices of a self-evidently wicked kind, while conforming to a reasonable degree with the circumstances in which his karma has placed him. In earlier times, when vocations were more clear-cut and also religiously guaranteed, discrimination was relatively easy though by no means infallible in practice. Nowadays, with the bewildering complications which beset almost everybody's life in the modern world a man can but do his limited best to conform to the ideal prescriptions of the Eightfold Path under the two headings in question; there is no call for him to scrape his conscience by looking far beyond what lies obviously within reach of a human choice. This does not mean, of course, that one need have no scruples as to what one does or does not undertake; where discernment is still possible, it should be exercised in the light of the Buddha's teachings.

8 By way of concordant testimony one can profitably recall the teaching of the great medieval Sage of Western Christendom, Meister Eckhardt, when he said that in the human soul 'is to be found something uncreated and uncreatable and this is the Intellect'; to which he adds that were it entirely such, it too would be uncreate and uncreatable. Substitute 'Bodhic Eye' for the word 'intellect' and you have there a statement any Buddhist might understand. In the traditions issuing from the Semitic stem, where the idea of 'creation' plays a dominant part, to say of anything that it is 'uncreate' is the equivalent of 'beyond the scope of samsaric change'. It should be added that, at the time when Meister Eckhardt was writing, the word 'intellect' always bore the above meaning, as distinct from 'reason' which, as its Latin name of *ratio* shows, was a faculty enabling one to relate things to one another apart from any possibility of perceiving their intrinsic suchness, which only the Intellect is able to do. The modern confusion between intellect, reason and mind, to the practical emasculation of the former, has spelt a disaster for human thinking.

The above example can be paralleled by another, taken this time from Eastern Christianity, where it is said that the crowns of the Perfected Saints are made out of 'Uncreated Light', or, as we might also say, the diadems of the perfected Bodhisattvas are made from Amitabha's own halo.

9 My friend Dr Inagaki Hisao has supplied a quotation from Shinran's teachings as embodied in the *Tannisho* (Chapter II) where the same sentiment is expressed consonantly with Jodo tradition and using its typical dialect: 'I would not regret even if I were deceived by Honen and thus, by uttering the *nembutsu*, fell into hell. . . . Since I am incapable of any practice whatsoever, hell would definitely be my dwelling anyway.'

VII

Dharma and the Dharmas*

as principle of inter-religious communication

The word *dharma* which the Indian traditions have rendered familiar has no really adequate counterpart in the terminology of European languages; if the range of ideas this word stands for must needs be found, at least implicitly, in the substance of every religion, absence of a readily intelligible term to cover that range in all manner of contexts remains a sad drawback as far as communication is concerned. Today one is feeling this lack more than ever, because the truths to which dharma corresponds in the field of metaphysical ideas and of spiritual and even social applicability are among the ones which, by the questions they raise, are troubling people's minds most acutely at this moment. This is especially true of the Christian world, where the question of formal incompatibilities between one religion and another, as against their mutual corroboration at a deeper level of understanding, has become a burning one; so much so that the credibility of Christianity as a way of life has become largely dependent, for many thoughtful followers of that tradition, upon a recognition of the dharmic principle as applying to interreligious relationships as well as to other matters of a less obviously controversial kind.

It was René Guénon who, writing in the 1920s, first brought to the notice of non-specialist readers in the West the fact that dharma, by virtue of its root-meaning, provides a ready-to-hand dialectical instrument wherewith to associate essential and accidental, being and becoming, in one single comprehensive vision of Reality. As he pointed out in his first major work, *Introduction to the study of the Hindu Doctrines*, the root *dhr* from which the word *dharma* is

*Essay written to mark the centenary of A. K. Coomaraswamy

102

formed enshrines the idea of that which stands in its own right as an intrinsic self-sufficiency; the sacred oak of the Druids (cf the Greek *dhrys*), as also their own name, stands as a joint reminder of this primary truth.

Starting off from this initial meaning carried by the Sanskrit root one can therefore say that *dharma* when unqualified (*nīrguna*) corresponds to the Suchness of Things; this is its message at a universal level. Passing to the level of particulars, dharma corresponds to that which makes any given thing to be such as it is, and not something else; this is true of things even when involved in the flux of existential change, *samsāra*; 'mode of being' here provides an alternative rendering of the basic idea. From all of this it can be seen that the same term *dharma* serves the double purpose of expressing the principial non-duality and the empirical duality of things; it is equally appropriate to the realm where oppositions do not (because they cannot) arise and also to the realm where, on the contrary, oppositions can and therefore must arise: the latter is the realm of distinction and change, of becoming, with all the shifting ambiguities which such a state comprises for us men and for all our fellows in existence be they great or small. If Dharma corresponds, on the one hand, to the absoluteness and infinitude of Essence, the dharmas for their part correspond to the relativity and contingency of the accidents. It is not without justification that in the sacred literature of Buddhism one frequently comes across the expression 'multitude of dharmas', which when transferred to a Western language will be appropriately rendered by the phrase 'multitude of beings'. To identify a being with its own suchness does not imply any logical shifting of one's ground; the dharma of each being covers it both in principle and fact, in essence as also across all the vicissitudes of its possible transformation – hence the manifold uses of this amazingly self-explanatory term.

Dharma, in its pristine immunity to any trace of restrictive distinction, is properly describable as void (*shunya*), while comprising *rupa*, form, among the indefinitely varied aspects and consequent relations to which its own non-duality gives rise, though without the least addition to, or subtraction from, its own imperturbable reality. As one of the properties of existence, form has been aptly defined as 'the appearance of a limit'. Body is a form, so is a world (ours or any other), so also are the various objects we encounter within that world and even in the realm of dreaming; each form displays its limits to an observer via the appropriate senses, including the thinking mind. The formulations of a religion, offering themselves to the mind, cannot altogether escape the typical limitations of form as such even while serving as means of approaching truths which *per se* transcend all form; a religious dogma is a case in point, being a form which, as such, at once reveals and limits the truth it is intended to safeguard for the sake of posterity. Wherever samsaric existence is in question, *rupa skandha* will belong in some degree or other, but so also will the other four skandhas, whether explicitly or else as latent possibilities.

This last proviso is important in showing that the possibility of salvation conventionally ascribed to 'sentient beings' does not really imply, as might seem at first sight, the existence of other classes of beings supposedly afflicted with a total inertia or, as one could also say, with an invincible ignorance excluding them altogether from the saving grace. A state of pure privation in respect of the vital Intelligence is not a possibility of existence. Every extant entity, however limited or lowly, will participate after its own fashion in the all-embracing suchness of the Real and therefore also in an ultimate possibility of nirvanic awakening via a human birth; it is no fiction to declare that at the centre of each grain of dust a Buddha is to be found seated and, as it were, waiting for release. When Jesus Christ said that 'if these [unperceptive men] should be silent, the very stones would cry out' he was not giving utterance to a picturesque allegory by way of making his point; he was pointing to the literal fact that each thing to be found in Creation may on occasion be called upon by a merciful Providence to bear witness to a truth which man, its normal spokesman, has neglected to notice at the proper time. This possibility is one which the Amerindian tradition has turned to the most positive account; for the indigenous inhabitants of the Americas the whole of Nature is like an ever open sutra in which may be read the multiform message of the Great Spirit. The dharma of forms is like a science of interacting reminders, the faculty for which has gradually been allowed to atrophy under pressure of ever-increasing sophistication. To retrain oneself to read the signs of Nature daily and hourly after the manner of the Red peoples amounts to an *upāya* of great power and subtlety, one which moreover is never far distant from that spontaneous compassion with which *upāya*, as *prajñā's* providential helpmate, is traditionally credited. Such is the dharma of natural forms.

When a being is manifested under a human form it will obviously participate in those affirmative but limitative conditions which pertain to all formal embodiments alike, regardless of species; it is expedient to note this general fact, as a prelude to considering that side of dharma which concerns us most immediately, not only as human beings but also as particular beings within the common category of humanity. The subject falls under two headings, individual and collective, each of which carries dharmic implications of a momentous kind. Intermediate between these two stands dharma as affecting the family; since the latter, like the dharma of an individual, is directly linked with biological necessity, it evidently occupies a place closer to the individual than to any group-interest even while sharing some features of the latter. The Confucian tradition as summed up ritually in the cult of ancestors constitutes an ethical commentary on family dharma unsurpassed in precision and depth of insight. Analogous institutions focused on man's membership of a family are, moreover, to be found all round the globe; whether one is dealing with the various tribal civilisations or with religions enjoying a world-wide scope one meets the same insistence on parental and filial relationships and their extensions into other degrees of kinship, as also on the necessity for the pious observation of family duties as an important feature in the pursuit of dharma. Nevertheless, there is something about a human individual which transcends all considerations of group-interest; a man's *svadharma*, that which corresponds to his or her own uniqueness as a person, counts before all else in the human scale of values; functional suchness with its attendant obligations as shared by others only applies at one remove. Existential exposure to the passing stresses of samsāra makes no difference in this respect; the changes one undergoes while being carried along by the stream of finite existence are evidently reflected in one's dharmic potential at any given moment. If the Buddhist view of this matter is relatively more dynamic than that of the Semitic traditions this does not in practice affect one's experiencing of *svadharma* as personal suchness or vocational opportunity in a very vital sense.

The concept of 'vocation' as coinciding with the dharma of a human individual will normally comprise three principal factors, namely a goal, a direction, and a path; in order to follow this path in the required direction with a view to reaching the goal we need feet to carry us and eyes with which to spy out the way as we go along: in Mahayana Buddhism these eyes have been likened to wisdom (*prajñā*) and those feet to method (*upāya*); all that pertains to human behaviour in this life comes under this twin control. By extension, the nature of method has usually been qualified by assimilating it to compassion (this was mentioned before), whereby are meant the attitudes and concordant actions expressing the relationship between the empirical self-consciousness of a being and all else that shares its capacity to suffer: by its twofold derivation the word 'compassion' expresses these two experiences, namely sharing and suffering. The association of ideas, wisdom-method-compassion, is of course common to all Buddhist schools regardless of local peculiarities; questions of phraseology apart, the Theravadist and Mahayanist teachings offer unanimous testimony in this respect.

For all those involved therein samsaric existence spells a state of fragmentation alien to selfhood – all that we feel ourselves to be or to own is *anattā*, could we but know it. Trying to gratify the insatiable appetites which we mistake for proof of our own selfhood brings us into conflict with others similarly affected and thus we all suffer together. Compassion marks our ability (and willingness) to see ourselves in the place of others and vice versa and to act accordingly within the limits set for us by antecedent karma, whereby is determined, for each being, its respective field of dharmic opportunity. This field defines our vocation, as *svadharma*, at any particular time or place in the cosmic scheme. Thus one can say that a man's *svadharma* amounts to something like a provisional suchness during this life, comparable to self-creation; indeed it is no accident that the two words 'karma' and 'creation' derive from a common root.

For a human individual to identify himself consciously and consistently with his own dharma while using those tools with which anterior karma has endowed him is self-evidently a crucial necessity which, if duly complied with, will imply for that person the realisation of all those possibilities which life itself has brought within reach. Plainly, a man's *svadharma* is inescapable as such; he does not choose it, it has already chosen him by force of pre-destination, as one might say. For us as men, choice during life lies between accepting our own dharma in a mood of passive heedlessness or else with mindful and active commitment at every turn, which is what 'a human birth hard of obtaining' is really for: one who does so will thereby be setting an example of the only kind of humanism worthy of the name.

The word *dharma* has often been translated, according to context, as 'teaching', 'law' and even as 'morality', a concept which will necessarily comprise both its positive and negative expressions; one will be taught that certain propositions are true and others false or that certain activities are lawful and in some cases obligatory while others are taboo, forbidden. This positive–negative antithesis holds good for the world regarded as a whole as well as for particular sections thereof; this opposition can even be applied to the whole of creation consonantly with the Semitic perspective, as also to the samsaric process in all its indefinite variety if an Indian religion be in question: to speak of 'a world' is to denote a play of contrasts; the word means nothing else, though details may differ endlessly.

For a world to come into being at all, the principial Unity which *per se* is without parts will paradoxically appear as if fragmented; whether one envisages such a happening in the guise of a divinely willed creation *ex nihilo* or as a manifestation without specifiable beginning as Buddhism has it, the resultant picture will not be so very different; that is to say the ever-varying components spawned by existence, if on the one hand they complement one another and incidentally affirm the overriding unity (this is their positive message), will on the other hand unavoidably compete with one another through their struggle to realise their own separate identity, thus masking the aforesaid unity (this is their negative effect). In other words, each being by its own existence willy-nilly imposes a certain restriction upon our vision of the One while at the same time, as a corollary, imposing a greater or lesser restriction upon the freedom of every other being; two beings cannot, as it were, simultaneously occupy the same metaphysical living-space; could they but do so, they would be one and the same being. This is a fact of existence into which it would, however, be a mistake to read a quasi-moral stigma except in the single sense that, but for this shadow of dualistic negation mutually cast by beings in relation to one another, no such thing as evil would be conceivable. No paradise without its serpent; but also no hell without its divine reminder: the traditional iconography showing a Buddha-figure standing in each of the six compartments which between them make up the Round of Existence, *bhava chakra*, (hells not excepted) is profoundly realistic as well as merciful, let us take comfort from this.

Once it is clearly recognised that existential diversity, itself ever on the move, will imply a corresponding dharmic diversity in which all beings share, it will thereby become apparent, in agreement moreover with what had already been said on the subject of dharma, that no two beings can take an identical course back from their peripheral state of dualistic doubt and servitude to the liberty and certitude only to be found at the luminous Centre of all things, that centre which is everywhere, as Pascal sagely remarked. In so far as we speak here of an awakening to, or attaining of, enlightenment, this will always remain an unparalleled happening defying all our samsaric eloquence to describe it. Even a Buddha when speaking to a samsarically entangled mankind will properly resort to human language in order to communicate the saving message; his hearers will take as much as each is able to understand at the time since, here again, diversity must prevail as in all other circumstances.

This rule of diversity as affecting all samsaric experience means, among other things, that no two beings will be governed by an identical moral law. For each being, its opportunities and its power to cope with them, as also such duties and rights as go therewith, must needs differ somewhat from those of its fellow beings even if, broadly speaking, the differences in question seem virtually non-existent to the onlooker: hence the inflexible character attributed to their moral codes by the various religions, especially in matters of emphasis. Nevertheless there is a distinction to be made between 'virtual' and 'absolute' which must not be lost sight of when considering what dharma means to us individually, as distinct from collectively. One is not impugning the authority of a law as traditionally recognised when one says that there may be occasions when it simply will not work and when, for all one's sense of obedience, one cannot avoid the conclusion that a more deep-seated justice forbids one to apply the law just as it stands. Jesus Christ, for one, was often at pains to point such discrepancies between letter and spirit in the face of the strongly legalistic bias of contemporary Jewish feeling. The exception that proves the rule must needs have its place in human awareness on pain of reducing everything to a flat and heartless routine; the rule itself would in fact remain incomplete without it. To recognise such an exception where this presents itself to one's intelligence falls within the purview of a man's *svadharma* on occasion, though prudence also requires that one be reasonably sure of one's own motives in thus diverging from the common law; the operative word here is 'mindfulness', the unremitting practice of attention which, for its part, includes a readiness to view an inconvenient truth without flinching and to act accordingly. Mindfulness is the Buddhist virtue *par excellence*; without it even compassion becomes unsure of itself. As one bhikku put it, there is no virtue but one can sometimes have it in excess, save only mindfulness; of this one can never really have too much.

There is one other aspect of dharma, a negative one this time, which concerns us humans intimately inasmuch as it is the quasi-divine gift of free will inherent in the human state itself which raises, for us, this issue: this is the possibility of *adharma*, or, in other words, the refusal or neglect of that which our human vocation renders incumbent. Obviously, our own nature remains such as it is in fact and so in principle does our dharma, but wherever individual volition is able to operate in relative freedom, there the responsibility will be ours, for better or worse. Such is the awesome liability attaching to man in function of his prerogative as the being directly eligible for enlightenment, whether he cares to appreciate what this means or not. For other creatures, experiencing their dharma for the most part passively and instinctively (but with a perfection of skill which, for us, could be a lesson), the adharmic possibility remains inoperative except as a result of human initiative such as all too often takes on monstrous forms. Such interference apart, one must also take account of the fact that the state of any world is itself closely bound up with the state of its central being at any given time, in which all lesser beings cannot but share indirectly; man's active and conscious realisation of his dharma, on which human primacy rests, imposes this condition on all who exist in his company. When Buddhas walk the earth all creation sings for joy; when man lapses into *adharma* he drags everything else down with him. The whole cosmic drama is ever being played out between these two extremes.

Dharma and the dharmas, unitive suchness and the suchness of diversified existence: here is to be found the basis of an inter-religious exegesis which does not seek a remedy for historical conflicts by explaining away formal or doctrinal factors such as in reality translate differences of spiritual genius. Far from minimising the importance of these differences in the name of a facile and eventually spurious ecumenical friendliness, they will be cherished for the positive message they severally carry and as necessities that have arisen out of the differentiation of mankind itself. Where the Semitic theologies, for example, out of a wish to safeguard the Divine Transcendence at all costs, appear to endow the world and its phenomena with what amounts to a quasi-absolute yet non-divine reality whereas the Indian religions, with their more graded approach to things, tend to attenuate the reality of the world almost to vanishing-point, one has to be able to discern, across the various incompatible statements, the genuinely intellectual motives which they respectively translate; it is neither right to accuse the Semites or their Christian fellows of accepting a radical dualism amounting to an unbridgeable rift in the Real (many pious souls admittedly do think that way, however), nor is it fair to see in a Hindu and more especially in the Vedantic view of the world nothing better than a monistic or pantheistic subterfuge of a mentality much given to metaphysical day-dreaming. History of the religions is full of passionate debates which amount to little more than two soloists trying to shout one another down; the long-term results of this sparring in the void can only be properly interpreted by facing up squarely to the various factors actually at play – intellectual, psychological and even ethnic in some cases. Saying this does not mean that one is out to explain religious differences in purely anthropological terms, that is to say by bypassing their significance as pointers to particular aspects of truth – unless indeed by 'anthropology' is meant not the profane medley now going under that name but a science founded upon the prior recognition of what it really means to be a man, *anthropos*, or, in other words, recognition of one's own dharma *qua* human being and of what this entails for all who have been qualified by birth into the human state.

Given that such an assessment of factors calls above all for a spirit of impartiality (which does not mean cynical indifference), one has to admit that such an attitude to people of other faiths finds more precedents in the Indian or Far-Eastern historical record than among the more sentimental and therefore also more partisan mentalities that grew up in the West. A long-established recognition of the principle of *svadharma* as applying to individuals, natural groups and whole religious communities has not only made for open-mindedness in respect of foreign doctrines and modes of worship but also has favoured what is often described, rather inappropriately, as religious tolerance, in the sense given to that phrase by liberal thinkers of the nineteenth century and after. To tolerate the opinions of other people does not necessarily imply respect; it can also go hand in hand with a neutrality not untinged with contempt: the emphasis here is subjective, it relates to a supposed right to hold whatever opinions one pleases, be they even the most foolish; an objective appreciation of those opinions as such hardly enters in. Such an assessment is poles apart from the idea of *svadharma*.

One of the most striking applications of this principle as criterion of qualification for specific functions and therefore also of position in a social hierarchy has been provided since early times by the Hindu system of castes. Given the fact that this institution has come under increasing fire in recent years because of various abuses (both real and supposed) which have developed as time went on – the common fate of all societies – it will doubtless come as a surprise to many to be told that the Indian 'tolerance', which Western people have tended to admire out of reaction against their own rather bigoted past, is itself largely a byproduct of habits and attitudes fostered by the caste mentality as such. For people who took it for granted that differing human groups, whether religious, racial or professional, would and indeed should have their own special ways of worshipping (affecting even the form of their deities) and their own customs and rules of conduct, coupled with the habit of marrying only within the ranks of their own community, it came natural to let foreign settlers in India carry on in their own ancient ways in proximity to the Hindu majority around them. The Parsee refugees from Iran following the Arab conquest of their country, the Malabar Jews and Christians all three provide examples of how Hindu habits of mind have operated in favour of perpetuating minority communities as distinct ethnic and religious enclaves instead of trying to 'integrate' them under calculated pressure as nowadays happens in professedly liberal societies such as Britain and the United States.

In fact, these minority groups in India have functioned down to our own day like so many subcastes; their cultural freedom, coupled with the conservation of their peculiar qualities, they owe entirely to the principle of *svadharma* as generally applied in the Indian world. Elsewhere such groups would more often than not have been eliminated, either peacefully through gradual inter-marriage with members of the majority or else forcibly, by persecution or expulsion, as happened to the Jews and Muslims of Spain during the sixteenth century. It is the glory of India to have found a way of accommodating those otherwise defenceless communities under conditions honourable to all parties concerned, thus incidentally preserving precious elements of variety which otherwise would quickly have been swamped. There is much to learn from this example, not only in a social but also in an intellectual and spiritual sense.

In a similar connection the Chinese record also has much to teach us. The word *tao* (literally 'way'), which has given its name to the Chinese tradition under its oldest indigenous form, bears a meaning analogous to that of *dharma* both in its plenary sense of the Nature of Things and in respect of its various applications. The following narrative will lend point to the above assimilation. In the year AD 638 a party of Syrian Christians belonging to the Nestorian sect reached China, and the question arose whether these new-comers from a distant land should be allowed to establish a centre in the country or not. The T'ang Emperor T'ai Tsung, after scrutinising the evidence submitted to him by his officials, issued the following Imperial Rescript which in its way might be regarded as summing up all the essentials of interreligious understanding, it runs as follows:

The Way [tao] had not, at all times and in all places, the selfsame name; the Sage had not, at all times and in all places, the selfsame human body. Heaven caused a suitable religion to be instituted for every region and clime so that each one of the races of mankind might be saved. Bishop A-lo-pên of the Kingdom of Ta-ch'in, bringing with him the Sutras and Images, has come from afar and presented them at our Capital. Having carefully examined the scope of his teaching, we find it to be mysteriously spiritual, and of silent operation. Having observed its principal and most essential points we reached the conclusion that they

cover all that is most important in life . . . this teaching is helpful
to all creatures and beneficial to all men. So let it have free
course throughout the Empire.

As a manifestly impartial tribute to the Christian religion could
this be bettered?

Latter-day China long remained faithful to the example set by
that noble T'ang Emperor, a man who richly merited his title of
'Son of Heaven'. Somewhere I have read a description by a traveller
who visited the parts of Szechwan and Kansu provinces bordering
on Tibet in which he tells how strangers meeting casually at an inn
after a long day's trekking through the magically beautiful country-
side were wont to greet one another. One man would say to the
other, 'Please inform me, Sir, of which sublime tradition are you a
follower?' The answer could be various; one man might say 'I go
the way of Islam', since there were districts of that region largely
inhabited by Muslims; the next man might answer 'I am an Insider'
(nang-pa, Tibetan for Buddhist); while again a third man,
recognisably Chinese, might say, 'For our family Confucius is the
rule of life, but we are also followers of Tao, the Way.' Whatever
the answer, it would be greeted with delight by all members of the
company, not only out of politeness, but also because, if the form
of their several beliefs differed (as was expected), their hearts
remained at one outside the respective formal limits; for people so
minded a conflict of loyalties would have been devoid of sense.

The gist of the above remarks must not, however, be pushed too
far. Were one to put to one of these same people the rather pointless
question 'But which religion do you look upon as the highest?' he
(or any of the others) would unhesitatingly opt for the form to
which he was personally affiliated, not because he had ever tried
to compare the various faiths point by point (this would be something entirely foreign to the habits of these people), but because
such a mentality always tends to express itself in forthright and
uninhibited fashion; unlike ourselves, these people feel no urge to
rationalise their own position at every turn. They have what one
might describe as a spontaneous sense of dharma. If such people
are still relatively common in the Asian world even today despite
the ravages of secularist propaganda which few places have escaped
altogether, such are not entirely absent here in Europe either and
wherever one happens to meet one of them this unexpected

encounter with the normal and truly alive invariably causes one's heart to leap. There is no greater consolation in this life than *Satsangh*, companionship of the true.

Speaking from my own experiences in India and in Tibet prior to the communist invasion, I enjoyed ample opportunities for observing how this widely diffused feeling for dharmic values operated in practice both at a popular level and among persons of superior learning. When a foreign religion was mentioned in conversation for any reason the immediate reaction was invariably a favourable one; one's listeners remained, however, incurious about details; this also was typical. On the one hand one encountered a ready assumption that other peoples, known or unknown, would have a religion and that this would be both good in itself and suited to the needs of those who followed it, but on the other hand no particular incentive was felt to seek evidence in order to substantiate these happy expectations or else disprove them, as the case might be. Dharmically considered, this was no concern of my Indian or Tibetan friends, so it could safely be ignored.

In the Christian world the prevailing tendencies have worked the other way round, historically speaking. The old Jewish hostility to the surrounding heathen, whose proximity posed a standing threat to that unitary faith of which the Jews were the chosen custodians, was taken over under the New Dispensation and also re-enforced in the course of Christianity's prolonged struggle against the Graeco-Roman paganism during the first centuries of its existence; an instinctive suspicion of all that was not of its own vintage from then on remained dominant in the Christian mentality. On hearing of some remote country, perhaps for the first time, there was an almost automatic expectation that that country's religion, if it had one, would be abominable; by dint of repetition, this kind of prejudice became a built-in component of the Christian psychism, to which there were relatively few exceptions. Here again, no desire was felt to test one's own feelings through recourse to tangible evidence; in regard to what other religions taught or permitted, the most fanciful stories gained easy credence which lasted for centuries. In the absence of a Christian equivalent of *svadharma* there was little to appeal to by way of correcting these false impressions as handed from mouth to mouth.

Harking back briefly to the first centuries of the Christian era, one finds that in certain communities of western Asia, where Hellenic influences were strong, it was usual to include philosophers like Heraclitus and Socrates among the sainted predecessors of Jesus. The Hellenic tradition itself, though in decline by that time, still functioned like a distant offshoot of Hinduism as evidenced, among other things, by the important part played there by myths and epics; at the refreshing fountain of this ancient lore not only the common people but also sages like Plato and Plotinus drank deeply; for them this was a means of strengthening their own links with the popular mind and also of offsetting the rather too rationalistic trend affecting the classical Greek mentality in its later phases. Though Christianity, as continuation of the Judaic monotheism on a wider scale, obviously could not draw on such a source directly, reverence for the elevated teachings to be found in the Platonic writings helped to keep alive, in a Mediterranean society on its way to becoming christianised, certain precious traits of the Hellenic wisdom: the mystical tradition, which, in Christian theology, corresponds to some of its profoundest insights, owes much to this providential cross-fertilisation of Jewish and Hellenic elements.

A somewhat similar proceeding could be envisaged today; the vastly increased knowledge of Asian, African and Amerindian traditions now available thanks to some 150 years of assiduous scholarship in many fields, if examined with unswerving objectivity coupled with openness to truth regardless of who may have been its occasional spokesmen, should render the task of restating the principles of dharma in specifically Christian terms that much easier. This kind of intellectual adaptation was what René Guénon had in mind when producing his first great commentaries on Hindu and other Asian forms of spirituality; he spoke of the West (i.e. Christians) needing help from the East for the purpose of rekindling the faintly smouldering fires of its own wisdom: there was no question of merely trying to copy Eastern ways; to transfer a few eclectically favoured features from one traditional form to another can do more harm than good. 'The dharma of another is full of peril', says the *Bhagavad Gita*, a matter of incongruity between things which in their own dharmic context are indubitably desirable. What Guénon hoped for was that an intelligent study of the Eastern religions would act as a catalyst of a metaphysical awareness to which Western minds had long been strangers, but

he was also careful to point out that the forms in which that awareness would need to be clothed for the purpose of its wider
dissemination would still have to be Western in character and in all
probability Christian.

Though Guénon's early appeal failed to stir contemporary
Christian opinion, it still remains timely; it is never too late for
metanoia, for a righting of one's perspective in the sense of the
first step in the Buddha's Noble Eightfold Path, and this is true
even in a world which seems intent on self-destruction. Any
reawakening to dharma and its values, however and wherever
brought about, will always be to the good, bringing karmic
consequences sooner or later which all the combined forces of
the Asuras cannot prevent from ripening in season, rage as they
may.

One of the factors affecting the religious situation which René
Guénon was continually stressing was the existence, under every
possible confessional label, of two main categories into which the
spiritual life of mankind could appropriately be fitted for purposes
of valuation; to these he gave the names of 'exoteric' and 'esoteric',
being followed in this by other writers in the field, including the
present author. Of these two categories, the first corresponds
roughly to the formal structure of a religion as conditioning the
human individual and the finality he or she can normally aspire to,
while the second corresponds to the innermost vision of things, the
effective realisation of all that Jesus Christ meant when he said 'the
Kingdom of Heaven is within you'. To this second category
belongs whatever concerns an initiatic dedication with its attendant
practices, of which the spiritual master (call him guru, lama, roshi,
shaykh or staretz) is the presiding figure, as distinct from the
sacrificial priest, whose normal field is the exoteric part of the
tradition with its rituals, its dogmatic teachings with their scholastic
commentaries and its moral code. As a prime factor of illumination
open to all must also be mentioned the forms of piety (*bhakti*)
but these, as well as Sacred Art, occupy a somewhat ambiguous
position on the frontier between the more outward-facing and the
inwardly poised intelligence; in a sense religious piety belongs to
both. By way of criterion as to whether a person is more at home in
the one or the other realm one can start off by ascertaining whether
he habitually shows himself more sentimentally or more objectively
inclined when trying to pass judgement on men or events; if the

former, one can infer an exoteric bias; if the latter, an esoteric designation is more likely to fit his case.

In any case it seems sufficiently obvious that with an exoterically geared mentality, for which loyalty to a form (including its limitations which, however, tend to be overlooked) becomes the one and only test of orthodoxy, a partisan attitude versus other forms, though perhaps not quite unavoidable, remains only too likely; to know what this can mean in extreme cases one has only to think of the medieval Crusaders or the Muslim warriors who invaded India, sincerely pious people all. Who can remember Somnath or Nalanda without a tear? Detachment and impartiality go more naturally with an introvert view of oneself and the world, a view which furthermore includes an awareness of the inherent fragility of every form, however hallowed. For this reason Guénon was driven to the conclusion, in which he was not wholly wrong, that recognition, even in a partial sense, of the dharmic validity of foreign forms is only feasible for members of an esoteric minority, probably operating in secret, as he hastened to add. An exoteric organisation like the visible Church, so he thought, could not stomach such a proposition for fear of endangering the faith of the generality of believers who, by the nature of things, will be intellectually mediocre and correspondingly vulnerable to all kinds of error. A policy of extreme exclusiveness was the outcome of a wish to safeguard the average man's faith at almost any cost. That a defensive rigidity in the framework might itself entail the probability of an eventual cracking is a danger which an ultra-exoteric mind is always slow to appreciate.

In point of fact Guénon's arguments apply almost entirely to the Semitic group of religions; the typical pattern of a tightly knit and legalistically inclined exoterism belongs there. Of the Indian traditions and their far-easterly neighbours one can say that if they also perforce have their exoteric framework they make up for this by a quality of metaphysical plasticity which in itself is a great protection to faith, though certainly not an unconditional insurance, as can be seen by looking around the East today. Because Guénon had come originally from a Christian background it was understandable for him to emphasise strongly this idea of exo–esoteric cleavage as being something which, as he well knew, many would find difficult to grasp. When writing on the subject Guénon came near to treating his two spiritual components as if they were enclosed in watertight compartments, the one being accessible to the mass of the faithful and the other only to the chosen few. That such is not the case is proved by the fact that an esoteric knowledge, being *per se* unlimited in scope, is for ever overflowing into the rest of the religious body of which it provides the intellectual life-blood; in this sense it remains open to all and may be apprehended according to capacity at every degree of consciousness.

Taking Guénon's thesis now at its face value, one can say that it corresponds to a truth of considerable scope; from which one can go on and consider another truth which had lain unnoticed until Guénon began writing about it in what was perhaps his most original work, *The Reign of Quantity*. What he pointed out there was the fact that time and space do not constitute one uniform and therefore neutral continuum in which beings appear and events happen, as commonly believed, but are themselves continually being subjected to qualitative differentiation just like all else pertaining to samsāra; the implications of this cosmological observation on the part of Guénon are momentous, since this means that what is an inconceivable happening at one time and place becomes perfectly possible at another in virtue of a quality pertaining to time–space as such, apart from any other more determinable causes. What we need to understand is that the ocean of samsaric becoming is far from uniform in its distribution of change. There are times when various currents come together with a force that seems to be sweeping everything along in a certain direction, after which the tide may subside into a comparative lull, only to allow fresh tendencies to arise and gather momentum in their turn, and so on indefinitely. The science of Cosmic Cycles takes account of these large-scale oscillations: of one of these we now seem to be nearing the critical point, if indeed we have not passed it already. A wave of doubt seems lately to have come over the minds of men, threatening to displace the former obsessive belief in a unidirectional progress (call it 'evolution' if you will) towards Utopia or 'Point Omega', or is it perchance hell? What's in a name, anyway, when one is on that tack?

Now I am thinking more especially of the West, where the abstract idea of progress originated, though by now, like other Western beliefs, it has taken root subsequently in many other places. Nowadays one keeps running into people both old and young but especially the latter who, carried along by the present tide of self-questioning, reject most of the concepts on which the edifice of modern civilisation reposes in order to seek out fresh sources of self-knowledge in places where their parents and grand-parents would have seen nothing but quaint superstition. To think of Americans and Europeans turning in all seriousness to Red Indian seers or Tibetan lamas for instruction as well as to avowed anti-progressives of their own race and kind – some change, to say the least!

In the light of these happenings, perhaps one need not be too astonished at the fact that those very truths which, according to the Guénonian scheme, were regarded as an esoteric preserve have now become familiar aliment for hundreds of modestly gifted intelligences. What then has happened to the secrecy formerly associated with these truths? Was Guénon wrong in the first place or have relationships between the two orders, outward and inward, changed in some subtle way consonantly with cyclic changes in the cosmic environment itself? In principle, one can argue that things are not much altered, since the two realms in question, insofar as they correspond to different levels of perception, the one individual and the other universal, remain such as they have always been; what is no longer clear, however, is where the frontier between exoteric and esoteric is to be drawn, if indeed a set frontier makes any sense in this order of reality; probably this is where the mistake lay in the first place – not enough room was left for overlap and interpenetration in either direction.

Anyone wishing to understand the nature of the extraordinary situation which has developed around us in recent decades cannot do better than turn to the Gospel according to St Luke, chapter xii verses 2, 3:

> For there is nothing covered that shall not be revealed; neither hid, that shall not be known. Therefore whatsoever ye have spoken in darkness shall be heard in the light; and that which ye have spoken in the ear in closets shall be proclaimed upon the housetops.

In other words, truths which not so long ago were extrinsically inexpressible and called for prudence on the part of the few who were capable of facing them have all of a sudden become accessible and even necessary to every man of reasonably sound mind; he neither has to be an initiate nor a genius in order to grasp them, at least in an elementary sense; their ontological assimilation in a fully effective sense is another matter.

One such truth has provided a subject for the present essay, namely dharma as key to an understanding of the *Transcendent Unity of Religions*, to cite the title of Frithjof Schuon's first and now famous book. In former times this would have meant little to most people, whose exoteric horizon was severely limited to a single religious form; besides, even to hint at such an idea except under the seal of esoteric privacy would, in many European countries of the past, have been highly dangerous under existing laws. In the Indian homeland of dharma the climate of opinion was quite different. Now, however, the Western situation has altered in spectacular fashion, so much so that in trying to account for the present changes it is idle to suggest that for some mysterious reason people in the West have suddenly become more intelligent – there is not the slightest evidence for this. One has to fall back on the idea of a shift of cosmic balance as providing a far more plausible explanation of the facts. An advanced stage of the Kali Yuga or Age of Iron (to use the Roman equivalent of the Indian term) is the nearest one can get to an explanation in cyclic terms. Again and again one meets serious-minded Christians who say that unless this particular truth can be intelligibly integrated in the Christian perspective they will be forced to quit, if reluctantly. For these people, a Christian orthodoxy which, after dodging the mass of well authenticated evidence in favour of other religions, insists on precluding all belief in a unity shared beyond the level of forms is no longer viable. In medieval times lack of reliable information provided some excuse for prejudice, but we have no such excuse – for Christianity to survive, let alone revive, it must face this issue. It is here that the notion of *svadharma*, presented not as something exotic but rather as a previously latent truth belonging to Christianity itself which now has emerged into the open, could be the saving of many precious things.

Our world is needing dharma more than ever, both as an ideal it has come to lack and as a means of shaping and judging all manner of human actions. Such was Coomaraswamy's message to our generation; his dharma was to serve, together with some others, as its faithful spokesman. Our dharma it is to listen to that message and, better still, to live it.

VIII

Metaphysics of Musical Polyphony

The possibility of creating music made up of several melodious parts moving concurrently in close but ever-shifting relation to one another was a unique discovery of the European artistic genius; one may add, of the Western Christian genius, whose spirit this form of music characteristically reflects. Harmonic modulation, which is the other face of polyphony, has put at the disposal of composers over the centuries a means of great emotive potency which, when harnessed to liturgical uses, enabled them to match the moods of Christian piety, as suggested by the scriptural and other texts they set, in a most telling way; joy or penitent sorrow, triumph or resignation, prayerful expectancy or the profound insights of mystical recollectedness all found their means of stirring the hearts of the faithful in the tonal medium provided by the polyphonic style. One can speak here, without exaggeration, of a sonorous theology whereby the truths of the Christian religion may be conveyed directly to the intelligence of those who know how to listen, be they simple believers or more instructed persons. This is a dimension of knowledge where set learning, or else its absence, makes little difference.

All this fits in with Western theological and devotional trends; it was the function of a consecrated polyphony in its heyday to complement the Gregorian monody while drawing from it much of its thematic material. In this way the primacy attaching to plainchant as the traditional song-form of the Church was duly maintained and this remained the normal relationship between the two musical forms over many centuries. This was still true when the Tridentine fathers set about their task of overhauling the existing arrangements for Catholic worship; it still held good in principle, though much less so in practice, when Pope St Pius X issued his decree concerning church music at the beginning of our century.

Given the initial acceptance by the medieval Church of polyphony as a suitable ingredient of the Christian liturgical art, its eventual predominance followed in due course; every branch of music, whether classifiable as sacred or secular, vocal or instrumental, came into line, thus leading by and by to a situation where unharmonised music felt like an anomaly to the average European ear. Whatever may be one's value-judgements concerning the ultimate results of that first big innovation, it is still reasonable to put the question as to what might lie behind a development on this scale having a character so obviously alien to the common practice of the rest of mankind; if the Western European peoples of a thousand-odd years ago were led into adopting such a novel manner of making music, what made them do it? Such a departure from generally accepted norms which, everywhere else, remained wedded to monody with or without improvised variations of a more or less elaborate kind and the spectacular results that have flowed from that departure cannot merely be explained in terms of a historical accident; they must stem from some deep-seated metaphysical insights of which polyphony became the natural mode of expression. It is on these insights that the present essay is meant to focus attention.

If music consisting of several parts meant to be heard simultaneously has long since become a built-in feature of the Western sonorous art, our own lifetime has witnessed a vast recrudescence of interest in those periods when contrapuntal composition, the special science of polyphonic interplay, was carried to its highest perfection, namely the fifteenth, sixteenth and seventeenth centuries. Wherever such music is presented, in concert halls or churches, young people flock to swell the audience; better still, groups are arising on all sides whose delight it is to meet in each others' homes in order to carry on a musical dialogue taking this form. This urge to revive an ancient art for which our parents and grandparents, whose musical taste ran in quite different channels, had no particular use has been accompanied by a zeal for authenticity; whatever information could be gathered through painstaking and imaginative research has been eagerly collated – the idea of trying to perform this old music in quasi-modern style, while using modernised instruments, has become taboo for the present generation of musical enthusiasts, with few exceptions. This battle, in which the great protagonist was my own master Arnold Dolmetsch, has virtually been won, though detailed investigation of all possible sources of evidence continues unabated as more and more examples of lost music are brought to light, many of them dating from the time when the Cathedral of Notre Dame in Paris was still under construction. Opinions which Arnold Dolmetsch had expressed with extreme vehemence in the face of contemporary prejudice are now commonly to be heard from the mouths of young professionals as well as amateurs, voiced in matter-of-fact tones that go to show how far the struggles of the pioneering age have been left behind.

It is opportune to point out that the now generally accepted principle according to which each kind of music requires its own characteristic technique, and for this same reason may exclude technical procedures belonging to other kinds of music, itself marks an instinctive awakening to a truth of universal pertinence, one to which Mahayana Buddhism has given concrete expression with its teaching about the indissoluble partnership of Wisdom and Method as applying to the art of music as well as in other spheres. Its style, as well as the content of all such compositions as belong to that style, represent the wisdom aspect of a given kind of music; all that comes under the heading of techniques, including the apparatus these call into play, represents method. These two interests are inseparable, they complement and interpenetrate one another at every turn. Arnold Dolmetsch never failed to inculcate this principle when teaching, both by example and by the nature of his criticisms. As his former pupil I can say, with gratitude, that this experience under the tuition of a musical sage opened my eyes to many things I would otherwise have missed; later, when it came to my turn to teach, I continued to base my methods on what that great man had first shown me.

All these things together have evidently marked a big change in musical sensibility; it is not only one's taste but, what is more important, one's whole manner of listening that has been affected. Where a previous generation had chiefly admired works of long duration in which the component material was spread comparatively thin, the present generation has again learned how to listen in depth; a contrapuntal masterpiece lasting no longer than five minutes holds their attention in such a way as to leave them feeling that they have participated in an ample musical experience, they ask for nothing more. Both for performers and listeners their scale of musical values has altered radically.

One point which hitherto has eluded all but a few observers is the fact that there is no known historical precedent for such a far-reaching attempt at resuscitation of the musical past as we are witnessing at present all over Europe and even as far as America and Australia; it has been reserved for the twentieth century to think and feel in this way. Other ages had been content with what the music of their own time, supplemented by some residual material of relatively recent date, was able to offer; whatever had come before was simply allowed to lapse at its own pace, including its greatest masterpieces. Shockingly wasteful, as one feels minded to say, yet such was the way the authors of those masterpieces expected their own work to be treated when it came to the turn of their successors to take over. It must be admitted that there is a certain air of selflessness about this attitude. Here one is speaking chiefly of European music, where the idea of individual creation has played an increasingly prominent part in people's aesthetic appreciation ever since the rise of polyphony. In countries whose arts had remained on a strictly traditional basis such considerations were unlikely to count except in a very limited sense. The conscious cult of originality, with the man of genius as its accredited agent, became enormously accentuated in the European mentality from the Renaissance onwards; in other traditions genius could win recognition on occasion, but this concept did not become obsessive as eventually happened in the West.

The vast undertaking involved in the present revival of earlier types of music therefore appears in history as something of a paradox; one may well ask what has caused people in an age nourished (or rather starved) on the ideology of 'progress' to wish to repossess all this bygone music at the cost of so much effort and with every appearance of wishing to satisfy an urgent need. What do they sense in this music which they cannot obtain by other means? More important, what actually is to be found there? This is the essential question.

By all the signs around us we can safely guess that behind this whole story lies an unavowed attempt to fill the spiritual vacuum left by the flight from Christianity in the West; the fact that this music, as was pointed out at the beginning of the present essay, was a characteristically Christian creation – it is shared with no other tradition – makes it all the more likely that those who feel so strongly drawn in this direction are, did they but know it, responding to a homing instinct. We are thus brought back to what essentially is a metaphysical question; what is the message woven into the very substance of this music? More particularly, what is it that musical polyphony, that unique creation of the Christian West, is able to communicate to human minds and human hearts?

Like every genuine art, music provides an image of the Universe, at the level of 'the Lesser Mysteries'; when practised with this truth in mind, it will serve as a support of contemplation and the joy it incidentally evokes will be seen as a reflection of the Divine Bliss.

The suchness of God, inexpressible and unmanifestable in Itself, corresponds, in our human experience, to voidness or *silence*. When silence is affirmed, sound then takes birth: 'In the beginning was the Word.' Music comes out of silence, and into silence it retreats in the moment of fulfilment. The primary affirmation of this truth is recognisable in the keynote, whether actually heard or implied in what is first heard; the keynote remains, throughout any piece of music, as a reminder of the *Unity* from which all that is manifested or developed derives its existence; the keynote, as it were, represents the germ of creation, it is never absent in fact, as efficient cause, from all the effects it will subsequently give rise to. Those effects are all contained in the primary cause, just as that same cause is communicated across its every effect, cause and effects being in fact inseparable; the prototype of this relationship is the Divine Intellect, wherein all that God 'has created' or 'will create' remains in a state of permanently present actuality which things and beings, in the course of their successive becoming, at once veil and reveal.

What actually happens in the created universe we see around us and in which we are involved? This universe is characterised by the triple fatality of change, competition and impermanence; to speak of a world (any kind of world) is to speak of contrast or opposition, for distinction of one being from another inevitably imposes this condition; 'a world' is always a play of black and white, with all the intermediate shades of grey or, shall we say, all the changeful play of the spectrum. What then exactly happens when two or more beings are developing in the same world? These beings may either converge or diverge or, for a brief space, move parallel with one another (or almost so, since an absolutely parallel course is not a possibility) and this will from time to time bring the beings in question into contact or even collision. What happens then? In proportion as one being is carried along with greater force as compared with another, the latter will get pushed and deflected from its course till it is free to move again in its own direction; this fresh direction it will pursue until it again runs into opposition of some kind – perhaps this time its own impetus will prove the stronger and it will be the *other* being which will be deflected in its turn and so on indefinitely.

What does this picture suggest but a *counterpoint* which, by its continual interplay of tensions and releases, expresses that unity out of which all its constituent elements have arisen and which they are all forever seeking to regain consciously or unconsciously? The musical parallel is self-evident and it is this, in fact, which confers on contrapuntal music its strange power to move the soul. The rigour of the contrapuntal principle governing the music of the fifteenth, sixteenth and seventeenth centuries in Western Europe easily accounts for the tremendous effect which this kind of music makes on the performers and, to a slightly lesser degree, on outside listeners.

For instance in a fantasy for viols, or in the Church music of the period, what is it that typically happens? Silence is affirmed (therefore also broken) by the primary enunciation of a theme which evokes, from another player, either *agreement* (i.e. repetition of the theme in the original key or else in a related key) or *contrast* (i.e. reply in the form of another subject); but this very relationship, inasmuch as it introduces a duality, leads to collision at some point or other; the stronger part pushes the weaker off course until the sense of opposition (which is what a 'discord' amounts to) has ceased, only to give rise to another such opposition as the parts in question encounter fresh points of resistance in trying to cross the path of some other part or parts. The search for freedom goes on as long as this process continues; each relation of concord represents a relative and provisional freedom with its corresponding degree of comfort, but so long as there is a process of *change* no situation can remain comfortable for long; oppositions will continue to arise, with a consequent urge to resolve them: only by a return to the original unity, of which the lurking memory constitutes one's incentive to achieve that very return, can peace at last be found.

Just as in the world one finds uphill and downhill, the one imposing extra effort and the other allowing of relaxed movement, so in our contrapuntal scheme we find that the interplay of parts is such as to impose, from time to time, an increase of effort perceptible by the ear as a *crescendo* and vice versa: this impulse to increase will always start in a *particular* part, it is never due to an arbitrary ('heretical') wish to play louder. In contrapuntal music, *crescendi* and *diminuendi* are always expressions of musical logic, not of some individualistic or sentimental motive in the players. It is always possible to determine exactly in which part, and why, an increase or decrease in sound is needed, evoking in its turn a corresponding response from the other parts, until a collective climax results for such time as musical logic does not begin to reverse the tendency in the direction of more or less sound. The *discipline* of contrapuntal music is to heed the signs telling one what to alter at a given moment; otherwise one goes on as one is. This kind of music – it is the secret of its quality – is half-way between a science and an art: *ars sine scientia nihil.* In teaching this music one should from the start accustom one's pupils to see and feel things in this way; one induces the right way of seeing through concrete example – theory and application keep step at every turn, but it takes some time before one is in a position, as now, to sum up one's experience in terms of a coherent synthesis.

Similarly, that counterpoint we call 'life' is a search for a unity which, across all the vicissitudes of existence, is sensed as ever-*present*: only in a return to our existential keynote will peace be found. Temporary resting-points or closes there may be; each passing cadence in fact provides in its own way a micro-image of the whole process of resolving dualistic opposition into unity. Each note included in a cadence calls for a different kind of emphasis; certain notes have to be joined smoothly, others separated, while some have to be swelled and others diminished. For a group of players or singers, to shape a cadence just right is already a collective exercise in unity, a distant foretaste of a lost bliss.

In terms of the more static arts, God has often been described as 'the great Architect of the Universe'; in terms of the essentially dynamic art of music, He could with equal appropriateness be called 'the great Contrapuntist of the Universe', since 'creation', the expression of 'being' through 'becoming', also implies its corresponding Divine Name, as above.

A more succinct version of the same idea might read thus:

Counterpoint, whether musical or existential, affirms and illustrates the unchanging presence of unity across all the vicissitudes of multiplicity, as also the reduction of the oppositions consequent upon the process of change to that same unity in which the process itself is for ever taking fresh birth. This is the mystery of existence (or creation) which counterpoint, in terms of sound, serves to reveal. Hence also the manifold profit to be derived from its intelligent performance, for those 'who have ears to hear'.

IX

Anattā

Impermanent is the human being, prone to suffering, devoid of self:
this adage is eagerly repeated wherever the Buddhist tradition
prevails, be it in Kyoto or Colombo, Lhasa or Rangoon, Peking
or in some Kalmuk encampment on the Caspian steppe. The same
statement applies to beings other than human; that which they
feel themselves to be, across their continually shifting experiences
of the pleasurable and the painful, expresses a want of intrinsic
selfhood, not its presence. Within the common ambience of cosmic
flux, as often as various factors become provisionally associated, we
beings live an empirical identity of which we misread the signs:
the doctrine of *anattā* (deliberately I have used the Pāli form of the
word in order to emphasise its historical precedence) is primarily
designed as a means of clearing the human decks prior to a proper
reading of those signs. If other religions, starting out from quite
different premises, have tended to foster belief in a 'soul' conceived
as a self-subsistent monad, for Buddhists it is its strenuous denial
which is the starting-point of true awareness. Before a man can
effectively put the vital question 'Who am I?' he must anticipate
it with the answer 'I am not such as this'. A whole metaphysical
outlook with its accompanying dialectical expressions has grown
out of this reversal of the more usual order of axiomatic
assumptions. To associate with Buddhists of all degrees under
conditions of intimacy, in a Buddhist country, allows one to
perceive how a whole mentality has been affected by the presence of
anattā among the basic ingredients of its intellectual formation.

If the existential dream we are all engaged in living, with its
persistent urge towards self-affirmation, be that which binds us to
the wheel of birth and death in continually renewed succession, the

Buddha, he whose title of 'the Wake' spells emergence from that dream, has shown us, first by his example and after that by his teaching, that his own awakening is something open to us too, for which our present human birth provides a vantage-point; for other beings, peripherally situated by comparison with our central situation, a prior human birth is a necessity before they can follow the same path. Compassion for our non-human fellow beings in existence arises logically once this fact is clearly recognised; to withhold that compassion through refusing to face what the human privilege amounts to in the way of obligations is a form of obtuseness peculiarly apt to bring about a loss of human status. Buddhism has always been most insistent on that score.

Given the above considerations, can one then take it for granted that Buddhahood as such is but another name for selfhood? Plausible though such a conclusion may seem at first sight it suffers from the objection attaching to every attempt to reduce an apparent opposition by causing one of its terms to disappear in favour of the other for the sake of a specious unity. It must always be remembered that the Buddha himself has gone beyond all possible dichotomies including the one of *samsāra–nirvāna*. From his transcendent standpoint neither the opposition self v. selfless nor their eventual complementarism raises any question; only in a fully awakened awareness can this open-ended equation be resolved without forcing the issue.

The point of view of 'non-duality' is such as to exclude all monistic explanations: hence the reticence of Buddhism on the subject of whether nirvana comprises a true selfhood among its attributes. Rather does it leave one to find out what all this means while one is proceeding along the human path to which a favourable karma has given access. Long and painful experience has shown that cogitative and sentient beings, despite all manner of dialectical safeguards, remain all too prone to impose on the word 'selfhood' those egocentric preconceptions which, by definition, keep the samsaric dreamland peopled, and not the world of reality. A perfunctory commitment to some comforting formula or other is asking for trouble in the long run; in Buddhist estimation, to foster a habit of rigorous inquiry coupled with unflagging attentiveness is the best way to bring about self-awareness, whatever this may ultimately mean; this is a matter of 'traditional economy' such as belongs to each of the great religions and determines their differences. It is in reference to this factor of economy that one can explain Buddhism's 'non-attitude' to self, as also to God, for these two notions hang together. The epithet 'atheistical' as applied to their own religion by some neo-Buddhist apologists becomes patently absurd for anyone who has fathomed the valid motives underlying the Buddhist reluctance to indulge in dogmatic formulations couched in positive terms; the teachings about *anattā* are typical of the apophatic method which Buddhism favours.

Incidentally, it is worth pointing out that these same neo-Buddhist writers on their own showing feel much more at home with the modern sociologists, psychologists and with materialist thinkers generally, *nastikas* all or 'nothing moreists' as Coomaraswamy had dubbed them, than with the theists and believers in self whom they go out of their way to deride. If the latter seem to come under the heading of 'eternalists' in the sense given to the word by the Buddha, these people forget that he expressly defined the Middle Way as passing between those two positions: to favour the one at the expense of the other is to opt out of the Middle Way as such, but an urge to follow the latest ideological fashions has obscured, for such people, their feeling for what is, or should be, most characteristic of a Buddhist outlook.

On the historical side of things some have been inclined to attribute the *anattā* doctrine in its inception to a wish to counteract popular beliefs about the soul prevailing in parts of northern India about the time when the dharma was first being preached, some of which took on a crudely superstitious form. Even supposing that this kind of motive entered in occasionally, it is stretching probability to assign so trivial a cause to an intellectual phenomenon of such far-reaching proportions; the diffusion of the *anattā* teachings far and wide among peoples of differing race and culture together includable in the Buddhist family asks for something better by way of explanation than this rather naive excursion into topical anthropology. If *anattā* is to be contrasted with some alternative conception which barred its way, the latter must surely be sought in the Hindu tradition at its intellectual best, that is to say in the world of the Upanishads where that idea of a transcendent self which later became systematised in the Shankarian Vedanta is already enunciated in all essentials.

Among notable writers on the subject during our present century two may be mentioned as representing alternative positions, namely René Guénon and Ananda K. Coomaraswamy. The first-named came into prominence during the 1920s with two remarkable books about Hinduism, aimed at helping the West to recover a dimension of knowledge of which Christian theology over the centuries had lost track. The young Guénon's new-found enthusiasm for the Vedantic wisdom as expounded by the great Shankaracharya led him into dismissing *anattā*, and the whole of Buddhism with it, as little more than a heretical ripple on the ocean of Hindu intellectuality; his own failure to consult parallel Buddhist texts was responsible for a hasty conclusion to which, for a time, he clung obstinately. At a later date, however, an approach was made to Guénon by myself backed up by A. K. Coomaraswamy, whose lucid scholarship with its scrupulous regard for traditional authority Guénon greatly respected, with the result that he agreed to eliminate from his published works the offending anti-Buddhist passages, a decision for which one will never cease to be grateful. This was an episode of my early life to which I look back with particular thankfulness; without that experience behind me I doubt if I would now be venturing to handle a question as delicate as that presented by *anattā* in relation to Hinduism and the theistic religions generally.

As for Coomaraswamy, his own conclusions were the exact opposite to Guénon's since at the time of his greatest maturity his commentaries became strongly biased towards demonstrating the thesis that the Buddha's teachings about self-knowledge approximated in essentials to those of Brahmanism, despite certain differences of expression. Coomaraswamy's views on the subject developed in such a way as to minimise the intrinsic originality of the Buddha's dharma in the interests of a somewhat artificial Hindu universalism. In support of this thesis he weighted the scales in a distinctly question-begging direction by resorting to a visual expedient which modern European languages alone have rendered possible but which Oriental languages exclude altogether, namely by employing the two forms 'self' and 'Self' in order to distinguish automatically between the empirical self or ego, seat of illusory thinking, and the true or transcendent principle of selfhood towards which all contemplative experience tends. At a pinch, such a procedure can be justified if one is handling Vedanta or another such theme in isolation; but to introduce it into a Buddhist context is both technically improper and misleading in the long run.

Apart from the linguistic objection mentioned above, this trick of transcription suffers from the serious drawback that it eliminates the ambiguity attaching to the various ways of using the same word 'self', an ambiguity which is in fact essential to any proper discussion of this matter if only because it corresponds closely to our human experience. Who is the true self? Context alone is able to show which self is intended in a given case; this is as true of written formulations as it is of life. To anticipate arbitrarily on the conclusion by robbing the key-word of its equivocal character is but to fog the main issue further. Ananda Coomaraswamy and René Guénon were both great men to whom our generation owes much; if I have criticised them somewhat in the present instance this is because it has enabled me to emphasise the point about a certain indefiniteness affecting the word 'self' as commonly used, a fact which when mindfully envisaged on each successive occasion will itself become a factor of illumination, not the reverse.

If one pauses to scrutinise the term *anattā* more closely one cannot but be struck by the fact that the mere addition of the privative *a* to *attā*, self, does not do away with the need to be clear in one's own mind about what it is that one is so confidently professing to deny. When we say of a landscape, for example, that it is treeless or of a woman that she is childless this goes with the fact that we ourselves stand in no doubt as to what is meant by trees or children, as the case may be. In the case of *anattā*, however, this proviso does not hold good; common use of this term by Buddhists is not matched by actual knowledge of what it is that is thus being held up to discredit. The conventional answer is 'a personal constant', but this answer in no wise explains why Buddhists and non-Buddhists alike go on behaving as if their own personalities and those of their neighbours are proven unities destined to persist through all the various vicissitudes occurring between birth and death and even beyond; they do not live as if *anattā* were for them a reality. The problem of identity therefore remains in practice as baffling as ever, yet this does not cause Buddhists to abandon their belief in *anattā* – paradoxically it makes them cling to that belief more tenaciously than ever. By them, that belief is not felt as a negative one, despite the form in which it is expressed.

It seems indisputable that, for Buddhists of every school, the term *anattā* carries positive overtones; moreover, the emphasis this teaching has received throughout the ages is a proof of its spiritual importance for those who follow the Buddhist dharma both as an idea and as a practical factor in shaping people's lives. Those who have read the biography of Mila Repa,[1] Tibet's poet-saint and ascetic, will doubtless remember that the wife of Marpa, Mila Repa's teacher, bore the name of Dagmema, which in English corresponds to our word 'selfless' (*bdag*=self, *med*=without, *ma* a feminine termination), being in fact the exact Tibetan equivalent of *anattā*. Can one imagine a more extraordinary name to give a person? Dagmema herself was a deeply compassionate soul who did her best to comfort her husband's young disciple while he underwent the succession of harsh trials decreed for him by his formidable mentor as a purifying expiation of his previous crimes of sorcery and murder. It is customary for Buddhists, when giving names to their offspring, to choose some intellectual or moral virtue such as 'profound doctrine', 'undefeatable', 'goal-attainer', etc., all of which are readily understandable as indicating ideals; but 'devoid of self', here is a truly amazing choice which cannot but correspond in intention to a positive quality of the highest order. Two negatives placed together spell a positive result; it is evident that in this example 'self' bears a negative meaning by implication: if this be the reverse of what Westerners discern in the word 'self', this must not blind us to the alternative possibility, namely that our customary consciousness of self is itself deceptive and that it is through its divestment that a real something may be discovered, one which cannot be named as such lest this should start a new chain of illusory attributions in its turn. As the Tao-te-king might have said, 'the self that is named is not the real self'. Buddhist practice, in this respect, savours more of technique than belief, but its overriding motive remains evident enough.

The present survey of an admittedly elusive subject would be incomplete without some reference to what is certainly the most suggestive parallel with the *anattā* teaching to be found outside Buddhism, namely Jesus Christ's declaration that 'if any man would come after me, let him deny himself'. What is this self-denial to which Christians are invited? The word itself as commonly used has become so impoverished as to be near to contradicting the Gospel phrase from which it originated. Something one decides to do without for the sake of others whose need is greater than one's own is denied to an entity taken at its face value as one's own self;

there is no question here of scaling down the validity of that entity as such. Taken in the sense of a generous readiness to forgo one's disposable possessions in favour of others, self-denial belongs to compassion; there is no hint of repudiating selfhood here.

When one sits down to re-read the Gospel with attention one is left in no doubt that Jesus's words carry a much deeper meaning than a mere readiness to help the needy; the question therefore remains as to what exactly was being demanded of his followers by Christ when calling them to self-denial. A conventional reply to this question would doubtless take the form of saying that it is one's habitual egotism that is to be laid aside in the name of Christian love; such an explanation, though plausible as far as it goes, does not go nearly far enough, since it leaves out of account the vital matter of identity; if the self referred to here were indubitably real on its own showing how would it be possible to alter that fact through its voluntary denial or in any other way? As they stand, therefore, Christ's words remain mysterious; they go beyond what unaided reason is able to explain. According to all three Synoptic Gospels Jesus went on to say that 'whoever would save his life will lose it'. What again are we to understand by this second phrase of his? Surely this means that the human soul, if it intends to heed Christ's call, must prove itself by casting overboard all it had clung to in the pursuit of self-assertive satisfactions; it must accept to suffer symbolical death in imitation of the physical death Jesus himself accepted on the Cross; without that death there would have been no Resurrection nor could there be such now. The 'self-naughting' of the medieval mystics echoes the same idea; the *Cloud of Unknowing*, that treasury of early English mystical specula-tion, could fairly claim to be a Christian exercise in *anattā*: for 'resurrection' read 'awakening' and you find yourself on Buddhist ground. To steep oneself in thoughts of *anattā* till one's whole being has become permeated by its understanding marks, for a man, his triumph over that living death which was a samsaric obsession with his own selfhood. Such is the price which Enlightenment requires of us all. Rennyo Shonin (1415–99), one of the Pure Land saints of Japan, put this very simply when he said: 'In the Buddha's Dharma selflessness is essential.'

The practice of *anattā* extends to all that man is and all he does; ideas are no exception, since each idea at best is but a means conducive to illumination, provisional therefore and expendable once its particular purpose has been served. Such is the attitude of Buddhism towards all that is enunciated by the mind of man, or filtered through it; the law of impermanence governing every manifestation in existence precludes one from eternalising ideas any more than other things, though one may cherish them so long as they apply to intelligible needs. More than all other religions Buddhism is sensitive to the danger of categorical statements taken for proven truth; hence its preference for non-dogmatic techniques. To recognise that the set forms one's religion comprises, even the most hallowed, belong to *upāya*, providential means, reveals, not a militant relativism but a sense of realism in regard to one's own intellectual position not unlinked to compassion with regard to that of others. The Buddha himself made it clear that he did not wish his disciples to accept his teachings perfunctorily, simply out of personal or partisan loyalty divorced from active intelligence. In all these matters the key-word is mindfulness; not even faith is able to function safely if mindfulness be wanting. To treat a dogma not as a key to a given truth but as that truth in an unequivocal sense is to impose on it an ideological selfhood no humanly dictated formula can justly carry; dogma, like any other effective expedient for forestalling error, needs *anattā* to keep it in balance. *Upāya* and *anattā* are the two props on which rest what, rather ineptly, has been described as Buddhist tolerance; between them they act as a wholesome safeguard for faith by keeping intelligence on the alert, where dogmatism, the habit of absolutising traditional formulations, creates unseen dangers by entertaining in people's minds an illusory feeling of security in disregard of the instability which everything to be found in samsāra comprises by definition.

It has belonged to the genius of Buddhism to give rise to a large variety of schools (I try to avoid the word 'sects', though this has been commonly used) about none of which can it be said that it is not orthodox in the broadest sense; each of these schools has developed a 'psychic style' that is all its own, thus also determining the nature of its accompanying dialect of the spirit: diversity of interpreters, as the Prophet of Islam has said, is also a divine gift. This diversity incidentally shows how each doctrine belonging to the Dharma is able to be viewed from several angles without losing any of its intrinsic sharpness; like other teachings, *anattā* has lent itself to a wide range of applications consonantly with the mentality created by the various schools. An actual example is the best way of bringing home this point; let us then take Jodo-shin, the Pure Land school of Japanese Buddhism, and see how this view of things applies to the *anattā* idea in practice; with one of the other schools the application of the same principle would obviously follow very different lines. If the reader will momentarily hark back to the essay on '*Nembutsu* as Remembrance', the sixth in the present series, he will be reminded of the sharp distinction, running through all Pure Land thinking, between 'self-power' (*jiriki*) and 'other-power' (*tariki*), with the former figuring as an exclusively negative factor in relation to man's dharmic potential while the latter is equated with the saving truth leading to that awakening of faith on which all else depends. As the aforementioned Rennyo Shonin has said, one should trust the Other Power; there should not be an element of self (anywhere in Jodo-shin).

Such a writing off of self-power logically must go with a distrust of selfhood as such; the whole spiritual programme of the Pure Land school is in fact an expression of *anattā* as lived in this world or in any other. What is not self cannot but be other: this reasoning sums up the elementary position from which all else derives in natural sequence. The aim before us, under this scheme, is an awakening of faith in the Other Power as represented by Amida Buddha, the living principle of Enlightenment at once transcendent and immanent, who, as Tathagata, 'he thus come', is includable in the endless line of Buddhas, past, present and future.

Given that the person of the devotee, thanks to the *nembutsu* and its invocation, has become emptied of all preoccupation with a self supposedly his own, his heart is thus prepared to offer itself as an empty vessel into which the Buddha's life-giving elixir may be poured. What formerly had been taken for one man's selfhood, opposable to that of other beings, now becomes replaced by the compassionate presence of Amida Buddha with the incidental result that all other beings, both collectively and individually, are seen as one great family in which all are parents, all are children, all are brothers, all belong to all without distinction. Here evidently we have entered a realm where the classical dichotomy between *attā* and *anattā*, self and selfless, is no longer operative; Amida Buddha has taken all that burden upon himself. Seen through the eyes he lends us, the realities we still perceive as *samsāra* and *nirvana* have become 'fused but not confused', to quote Meister

Eckhardt's immortal phrase; this is the vision his compassion offers us under the symbolism of the Pure Land.

There is a story which gives an inkling of what a man is like who has come to live by *anattā* or, if you so prefer, by 'other power'. In relating this story a term will be used which belongs specifically to the vocabulary of Jodo-shin. This term is *myokonin*, literally meaning 'wondrously excellent', and usually refers to persons of simple appearance, considered naive by their more sophisticated neighbours who miss the fact that under a childlike piety a high degree of understanding can lie concealed; Jesus Christ's frequent references to receiving his teaching like a little child agree very well with a *myokonin*'s designation.

The story goes that one such *myokonin*, an elderly man, was travelling by a boat that plied from one Japanese island to another. In the middle of the night while most people were asleep a terrible storm arose; all the other passengers woke up in terror as huge waves imparted to their small ship an ever more threatening list, but the old man went on slumbering peacefully. After a time his companions could stand this no longer; while some seized him by the shoulder and shook him violently, others cried out 'Wake up, wake up, the ship may capsize at any moment!' Slowly the old *myokonin* opened his eyes and looked from side to side: 'Oh, I see,' he said, 'we are still in samsāra; there has been no change', whereupon he turned over on his side and dropped off to sleep again. Here was a man for whom *anattā* was no empty concept. Such men teach through their being; for them verbal arguments would be superfluous.

The foregoing discussion has necessarily followed a rather erratic course, if only because the subject of *anattā* does not primarily lend itself to systematic analysis and definition; a succession of discontinuous glimpses agrees better with its spirit. When all is said and done, *anattā* offers itself to our human intelligence as a supreme *koan*, an enigma which by constant meditation carried on in the stillness of one's heart may all of a sudden yield up its secret. It is for a Buddha alone to know what 'self' and 'selfless' really imply; for beings still dwelling on the hither side of Enlightenment a certain inconsistency of view cannot but prevail. This evidently is our position; we can only know certain things at second hand, by observing how others behave whose knowledge has matured further than our own. The *myokonin*'s story will help to point this moral.

In the face of *anattā* the question of identity remains crucial: who then is speaker, who is hearer? Starting from the Hindu end of the intellectual spectrum, *atmā-vichara*, self-inquiry on the lines inculcated by a great sage of our time, Sri Ramana Maharshi, converges on the selfsame question. Whenever people brought to him their personal or moral problems, instead of trying to elucidate them piecemeal as usually happens, he would lead back the inquirer to the most basic question of all, the one on which all other questions ultimately depend. If one may be allowed to transpose the Maharshi's phrase into Buddhist language one could speak of *anatmā-vichara* with equal propriety: here the Sanskrit has been preferred to the Pali form in order to throw up the parallel more sharply. Can anything more paradoxical be imagined than an investigation of one's own non-selfhood? (Who then is the owner, who is investigator?). Likening such an inquiry to a supreme *koan* was surely not inappropriate, besides the fact that the use of *koans* by the Rinzai branch of Japanese Zen would scarcely have been conceivable but for the *anattā* teachings; used as a means of breaking down the psychic adhesions created by an unrelieved dualistic habit, the koan-linked psychotherapy does in fact reflect those teachings in a manner agreeable to the mentality developed among Zen adherents in Japan, just as the seemingly very different cult of 'other power' in the Pure Land school reflects those same teachings in a no less characteristic way. So long as *anattā* remains a half-digested, half-obscure notion, as is the case with every non-enlightened mind, the need to wrestle with this question of identity will impose itself after the manner of a natural *koan* and this need, failing enlightenment, will last as long as life. In this respect, the assurance with which many Buddhists speak or write today about *anattā* is largely deceptive.

Typically, a *koan* has the form of an apparently self-contradictory question on which the Zen aspirant is invited by his roshi or spiritual master to meditate unceasingly till he has found a satisfactory answer; pursuit of this trying task may go on for years, punctuated by periodic meetings with the roshi, to whom his disciple submits such answers as may meanwhile have come to mind. More often than not he will be brusquely repulsed by his teacher, sometimes with a few blows added by way of encouragement, before being sent back to his meditation chamber to try again; until one day, without the least touch of drama, he will be told by the roshi that his answer is the right one. For us outsiders it would be a mistake to look for some discernably logical connection between the question as originally put and the successful answer; all one can say is that, to the roshi's intuitive power of reading his disciple's soul, that last answer of his is such as to prove that *satori*, illumination, has actually taken place. What in the absence of a better term we call an answer corresponds to an evocative allusion on the part of the disciple, revealing an experience occurring in a region of the human psyche quite other than that of ordinary thought and speech. This does not mean, however, that this evocation is itself a product of the psyche as such, but only that it has used the psycho-physical vehicle as a medium whereby to become apparent to the surface consciousness of the person concerned, as also to us as onlookers.

In terms of wisdom and method this use of *koans* as intellective supports is such as to justify one's describing them as 'mysteries', a matter of sense, not of etymology, since the syllabic structure of the word itself, as a Japanese expert has informed me, affords no clue as to how it became applied to its eventual use as a support for Zen meditation. One important thing to bear in mind, when discussing this subject, is that *koan* does not correspond to what we would call a 'riddle', that is to say an ingenious question calculated to baffle an average mind but which may eventually yield to mental powers of great acuteness: the famous riddle of the Sphinx, for instance, did not have the nature of a *koan* since neither the question as first put by the monster nor the answer given by Oedipus came outside the circle of rational thinking such as both the propounding and the solving of a *koan* exclude *a priori*.

If one would seek a certain parallel with the *koan* method it is still within Buddhism that this will be found. The Tantric initiations make frequent use of a type of formula called *dhārani*, literally meaning 'ground' (for invocatory meditation) rather like our own word 'support'; such a formula usually consists of a number of syllables strung together in apparently haphazard fashion, though without displaying the distinctive whimsicality of many Zen *koans*. Some of the syllables figuring in a *dhārani* come from the common vocabulary of the mystical tradition while others, as they stand, often seem barely intelligible. The initiating lama will present a given *dhārani* to his pupil before immuring him in his meditation cell (familiarly known as 'the palace') or else, if the pupil be the like of a Mila Repa, he may let him take up residence in some convenient cave looking out on a Himalayan glacier, there to await the time when, by dint of one-pointed concentration on the mysterious formula, this shall have revealed its arcane message. Here, as with Zen, there is no question of any analytical exercise on the disciple's part; rather should one speak of the catalysis of something in him which the *dhārani* also carries in potency: there is always an element of recognition, of meeting what is already there, in every awakening to the light of Bodhi; even in cases of a partial illumination this is true.

Today it has mostly been forgotten that the root meaning of 'mystery' is muteness, deliberate silence, either because one knows that the knowledge in question is too profound to be expressed in words or else that it is such as to spell danger for all except the most qualified initiates working under the close supervision of a master. Behind this silence a cause of another order is discernible in the fact that certain truths, by their very nature, stand in no need of distinct affirmation in order to convey themselves to any mind that is unhampered by craving for self-expression. It was Frithjof Schuon who, when shown my script, pointed out this unperceived factor affecting metaphysical communication, in which quasi-moral considerations of desirability or prudence play no part; on reading his remark I thought that this was too important a matter to leave unmentioned, so I hastened to make room for it in my text. Awareness that truth comprises, side by side with its capacity for revelation, such a quality of spontaneous reticence runs parallel with the knowledge of *anattā*; it matches an attitude of unconcern in regard to contingencies, thereby leaving room for a spirit free from self-obsession to make itself felt in human thinking and action. Action undertaken consonantly with one's own dharma but without attachment to fruits, whether by anticipation or subsequently, constitutes a yoga in its own right, one in which the commonly contrasted claims of contemplation and action are effortlessly reconciled. The Vedic tradition, speaking through the sublime poetry of the *Bhagavad Gita*, has given especial prominence to this synthesis of the contemplative and active lives. Buddhism for its part attacks the tendency to attachment at the subjective end of things by emptying an alleged selfhood of its apparent substance, leaving the fruits of action, at the objective end, to shrivel and drop off the existential tree for lack of sap. *Anattā* is the specific remedy for bringing about this riddance of a misjudged self-consciousness. True consciousness can be trusted to follow once the obstacles to an awakened intelligence have been cleared from the path.

Speaking in a more general way, it can be said that mystery, among men, is the methodic counterpart of paradox as pertaining to the order of divine realities which, for their part, constitute the sapiential fountain of whatever esoteric knowledge may be in question. In the Hellenic world where the word itself originated, the Mysteries, of which those of Eleusis were particularly famous, covered much the same ground as the initiations of Indian tradition; they represented the more inward side of the Hellenic religion for which the temple rituals and the public teachings of the philosophers between them provided an outward framework. When Christianity, some centuries later, came to replace the old Mediterranean religions long since in decline, it was only a step for the terminology of the ancient mysteries to be transferred to the Eucharist and other Christian sacraments; in the Orthodox Church these are known as mysteries to this day. The word 'mystical' as expressing whatever in a religion is most interior carries a similar implication of silence, of something too profound to be rendered adequately in positive terms. Hence the preference for apophatic expressions on the part of those who speak for the mystical theology: to deny whatever would tend to limit men's conception of the Divine is more conducive to its understanding than the carefully calculated statements of scholastic commentators. In this respect the Christian mystics, both eastern and western, have both dialectically and in practice come close to Buddhism and the other Eastern religions.

What is most characteristic of a mystery, whether presented in ritual form as with a sacrament or as a metaphysical proposition, is the fact that it can be highly productive in the life-style of those who participate in it without this fact necessarily implying any great degree of conscious understanding by those whose life it has fertilised to such good effect; more usually, the mystery works as its name implies, that is to say silently and in the dark, after the manner of a ferment the action of which the persons who stand to benefit would be at a loss to explain. Life as a Buddhist would not be what it is without the pervasive but largely inarticulate consciousness of *anattā*; it is normal for its truth to reach people as a rather fluctuating experience, like a flickering lantern perceived from afar by two friends (or are they unwitting rivals?) who have got benighted in a forest – at one moment their eye catches a distant glint, the next moment it has faded into the background leaving them bewildered. 'I think I see a light', says one. 'I don't see anything,' answers the other. 'There it is, can't you see it?' 'It must be a will-o-the-wisp!' 'No, there it is again, that is certainly a light, it must come from some woodman's hut where we can seek shelter – but no, whatever can have happened to that light? I feel sure I saw it clearly. It's gone, what shall we do now? I think I felt a drop of rain. Look, there it is again. Let's press on.'

If this little parable of one man's experience during his passage in the direction of self-naughting, together with the various comments that led up to it, shall have proved of any assistance to others bent for the same goal, the present essay will have been worth writing; otherwise not. Perhaps the most appropriate way to finish this very mixed commentary is by repeating the words with which it opened: *Impermanent is the human being, prone to suffering, devoid of self.* These oft-quoted words are no more than an amplification of the first of the Buddha's four Noble Truths, the truth of suffering, to which they add nothing essential. And as for grasping the fullest meaning of those words, this is reserved for any man who, following the Buddha's lead, shall in his turn sit down at the foot of the World Tree braving Mara's assaults while the Vaisakh moon, Amitabha's halo, pours down on him its blissful light. For such as he, *attā* and *anattā*, self and unself, will no longer raise a question mark; for us, many miles still lie ahead before we can do likewise. Or might it only be a few? Events will show. The great thing to remember is that the Bodhi tree is everywhere; any time is Vaisakh-time for the man of awakened faith.

NOTE

1 An admirable translation of this supreme spiritual document has been published by Clarke, Irwin & Co., Toronto and Vancouver, Canada. The translator is Lobsang P. Lhalungpa, one of Tibet's foremost scholars, who has also added an introduction which is itself a most precious addition to Buddhist exegesis. Another splendid translation (last part abridged) exists in French, by Jacques Bacot, republished by Fayard. Both the above translations are works of genius.

X

Archetypes, as Seen Through Buddhist Eyes

The word 'archetype', derived from two Greek roots respectively meaning 'origin' or 'principle' and 'fount', has attracted much attention in recent years as a result of its adoption by psychologists of the Jungian school, for whom it denotes a characteristic function of the 'collective unconscious'. Allowing for the fact that their use of this term has given it a somewhat equivocal twist, it can also be said that recognition of archetypal phenomena within the psychic order does not take one very far along the road of understanding what the word itself originally meant, and still must mean if it is to be fully intelligible; in an Aristotelian sense this restricted usage pertains, on its own showing, to the *physical* order, while leaving out of account the metaphysical realm where it primarily belongs. Whatever exists in a relative sense, as an element in the samsaric vortex, must needs have its corresponding place in the still waters of nirvanic consciousness; the colours of the spectrum find their synthesis in the uncoloured light of the Void, coming in and out of it as existential contingency may require; but, for all this scintillating interplay of light and shadow, they will still subsist there in the eternal present, as archetypal potency and actuality, the two in one. It was St Thomas Aquinas who said, when speaking of God, that for Him there is no difference between potentiality and act. This is good Buddhism – one has but to transpose the Angelic Doctor's statement into the language of the Bodhic dharma in order to recognise similar, if differently expressed, teachings.

By way of approaching our chosen theme, let us first cast back our thoughts to the traditional iconography of the Round of

Existence as outlined in the first essay in this collection. It will be remembered that this pictorial image of the Cosmos consists of a wide circle subdivided into six segments each of which houses one of the type-classes of beings, of which human beings form one. Encircling this main field we find a narrow band showing a sequence of small scenes each of which serves to illustrate one of 'the twelve interdependent causes of origination' (*pratitya samutpada*), ranging from *avidyā*, unawareness, to *jaramarana*, old age and death. Here one may recall the fact that the Buddha, on the night of his enlightenment, after tracing these causes one by one in the direction of their successive affirmation, then proceeded to run through them in reverse order, thus showing that the vicious circle of rebirth-redeath is able to be broken once true knowledge has come to fill the vacuum in intelligence left by unawareness; the process of awakening starts from there.

Set in the middle of the main design we find a smaller circle wherein are displayed the 'three poisons' in the form of a pig, a serpent and a cock biting each other's tails as they whirl round in ceaseless struggle for dominion over the minds and bodies of beings, with variable success, since predominance is never quite achieved by any of the three sinister contenders even if appearances sometimes suggest that such a thing has happened. The three animals in question respectively represent ignorance, aggression and desire-attachment; it is a combination of these factors, always shifting its balance, which will at any given time colour the character of whatever being one likes to name.

It is worth pointing out that these three existential determinants also figure in Hindu cosmology under the name of 'the three *gunas*'; Buddhism took over the *gunas* while imparting to them a slightly moralistic slant. In the Hindu version, *tamas*, corresponding to the Buddhist 'unawareness', represents the tendency to inertia, passivity, fixation; while *rajas*, the second *guna*, represents an expansive tendency, hence also aggressiveness when meeting obstacles to self-assertion; and the third *guna*, *sattva*, is likened to an ascending tendency, an aspiration in the direction of higher things – hardly suggestive of a poison except in the sense, on which Buddhism has fastened, that any existential entanglement as such carries certain negative implications. Desire may be egocentric or the reverse, but as a factor of attachment it remains equivocal.

As distinct from the negatively biased concept of three poisons, the Hindu *gunas* lend themselves to many applications in the sphere of practical concerns as providing a conveniently succinct criterion when wishing to describe the nature of any extant thing, be it an individual being or a species or even an artistic creation of the human mind and hand. One can, for instance, qualify a lotus as an eminently 'sattvic' flower; so is a rose or a lily, hence also their sacred associations in various religions. The same criterion, among minerals, may be applied to a diamond as well as to gold, whereas lead remains typically 'tamasic', a fact which explains the symbolic use of these metals by alchemists. Yellow phosphorus, on the other hand, is undeniably 'rajasic', it bursts into flame after exposure to the air for a few minutes. In medicine the three *gunas* can play a useful part in diagnosis; nor must one forget the manifold applications of the *gunas* in the field of diet. One common mistake made by those not yet familiar with this Hindu teaching is to regard *tamas* as tantamount to badness, by ignoring its positive quality as an essential factor of stability. Where would a Buddha's body be without *tamas* to give it solid substance? Indeed, where would the compassion of a Bodhisattva be without *rajas* to fuel his initiative? Perhaps enough has now been said to show how the principle of *gunas* works.

Returning to the Round of Existence as depicted by Buddhist artists for the instruction of men, it should be added that this pictorial image is always shown as gripped in the claws of the fearful figure of Yama, Lord of Death who, as agent of karmic justice, is indifferent to any pleas. That Yama is not a demon, but a god, is shown by the presence of a third eye in the middle of his forehead, representing the eye of bodhic discernment. Lest, however, the sight of this awesome form, on the top of all the other warnings entering into this design, should drive a timid beholder to despair, a note of hope is sounded by the presence, in each of the six compartments among which beings are split up, including the hells, of a Buddha figure as the compassionate witness of their vicissitudes and as reminder that the vicious circle of repeated birth and death can itself be broken, given a shift from congenital delusion to right vision. Call this repentance if you will, since this is the primitive meaning of the Greek word *metanoia*, inadequately translated by a word meaning 'to be sorry'; it is a change of viewpoint which Jesus, like the Buddha, proposes to men first of all.

The above description of the Round of Existence, classical for

Buddhism, is calculated to strike the human mind above all through its dynamic overtones; impermanence, change from one state to another, alternations of pleasure and pain, relativity of all we would fain treat as enduring, these form the message this symbolical portrayal is meant to deliver. The little insets round the outer border corresponding to the recurrently interdependent causes of origination in this world, together with the trio of animals interlocked in mortal competition at the centre of the picture, by their action upon the eye of the beholder help to reinforce this general impression of motion without any possible let-up. The famous saying of Heraclitus 'all things are flowing', sums up this situation; this is the very charter of *samsāra*.

After this rather detailed analysis of a traditional icon which faces one at the entrance of every temple of the Tibetan world, we can profitably pass on to consider an alternative model of the cosmic relationships, one that is much less generally known since it belongs specifically to the spiritual apparatus of certain Tantric schools. This second version of the Round of Existence (it is in fact known by the name of *mandal* after the Indian word for 'circle' shorn of its final *a*) has not been given pictorial form; its model has to be created in the mind and then dissolved and then re-created one hundred thousand times; the only concrete support used by those so engaged is a largish disc, often made of silver, on which they set out the various items of the prescribed scheme of creation by means of pinches of barley. Once their miniature cosmos has been duly constituted it is swept off the board and then begun again until the total number of repetitions has been reached. One could describe this as 'invocation in semi-visible form'.

When constructing this form of mandala the exercitant first places a pinch of barley in the centre of his disc to represent the axis, here assimilated to Sumeru, the mountain which in the sacred geography of India marks the mythological centre of the Universe; round this mountain, conformably with the four directions of space which are also marked· by heaps of barley, all known or unknown continents and countries are grouped. Within this broad framework more barley-corns are placed to show the position of the sun and the moon, together with other prominent landmarks. Last, more grains are dropped here and there to represent various kinds of beings. This completes the mandala. After contemplating his creation for a few moments the exercitant will then, by a brushing motion of his hand, clear all the grains away, leaving the bare disc ready for the cosmogonic drama to be gone through again.

By comparison with the flat and dynamically biased image previously described, this second mandala offers us a three-dimensional model carrying much more static implications. The concept of an axial mountain rising up from a broad and solid base and gradually narrowing as it nears the summit, coupled with the four directions of space of which it marks the intersection, suggests at first sight a pyramidal structure. The name of *mandal* given to this model would however seem logically to require a conical form; pyramid or cone makes no essential difference to the symbolism, which is one of existential levels, hierarchically determined in relation to the axis. Each level will therefore represent a mode of existence with its corresponding class of beings, while at the same time pointing to the nature of their common dharma. It is, moreover, self-evident that the higher up the mountain one climbs the smaller will be the area covered by that particular existential level; levels situated deep down towards the base will be correspondingly wider and therefore also more dispersive in regard to the beings which occupy them. The higher one goes the more concentrated will be one's manner of existing. The terms 'infernal' and 'supernal' used by the various traditional eschatologies owe their meaning ultimately to this distinction. Hell is terrible in function of its dispersiveness; its hot or cold comes afterwards. Heaven is blissful for the opposite reason. There is a state of being where one-pointed concentration is virtually self-acting; so close is the summit of the mountain as to be felt like an irresistible magnet. One who has reached this state is known as *anāgamin*, he for whom there is no return (into samsaric confusion); but at this point a question of level hardly arises.

Apart from the repartition of planes according to the spot where each cuts the central axis, with the broader valuation this serves to emphasise, another more particular scale of values can be established within any given horizontal plane in terms of proximity to, or remoteness from, the meeting-point with the main axis; in this manner the latter affirms its natural claim as the decisive criterion of existential discrimination. Symbolically speaking, it is the ratio between these two determining factors, the vertical axis and the horizontal plane which cuts it, that will serve to 'value' every being to be found anywhere within the same cosmic framework. It should not need pointing out that all these geometrical analogies are but *upāyas*, means of establishing valid points of reference and therefore able, when pondered mindfully, to impart a stimulus to intuitive perception; if a certain rationality appears to enter into this argument, the picture propounded for observation must never be confused with an attempt at scientific naturalism lest a double confusion should occur between things of a different order: this warning should be borne in mind.

Additional light can be shed on this question of cosmic correspondences by calling to mind two technical terms belonging to Islamic cosmological science, namely 'exaltation' (the direction of the vertical axis) and 'amplitude' (the direction of the horizontal plane which in its own way is also an axis). Between them these intersecting axes describe a *cross*; this is an archetypal symbol of major importance which its Christian use, derived from the events of Calvary, but serves to enhance further. A not far short of exhaustive commentary on the cruciform symbolism exists from the pen of René Guénon, of which an English translation under the title of *Symbolism of the Cross* was published by Luzac in 1958. The author illustrates his theme by means of numerous geometrical analogies which, in the absence of linear drawings, are not always easy to imagine by a reader who is not himself mathematically inclined; but in its main lines this treatise of Guénon's is readily intelligible. It was, moreover, followed by another treatise on the same subject, unlinked this time to mathematical concepts, which still lies untranslated. Its French name is *États Multiples de l'Être*. These two books might well be published under one cover, since they complete one another.

The great importance of Guénon's *Multiple States of the Being* lies in the fact that it demonstrates the possibility, in the case of any being one cares to select, of surveying all the episodes of its samsaric manifestations simultaneously, as in a single glance; the same will of course apply to any natural entity, be it a given world or even the whole of cosmic reality, provided the beholder's viewpoint be itself situated, at least imaginatively, high enough to look down upon the Axial Mountain from above; one could also have said, from a nirvanic viewpoint outside all considerations of time, space or direction. The word 'simultaneous', which has just been used, can evidently be replaced by the word 'present'; where there is succession there can be no presentness; *samsāra* is characterised by continual passage from potentiality to act, endlessly repeated. We who are involved in that process may speak of the present as something immanently sensed but never experienced as such; the idea remains, for us, an abstraction, but its reality transcends us. For 'present' one could also substitute the word 'eternal'; the phrase 'eternal present', highly suggestive and often used though it is, harbours a tautology. This vision of things is one that can properly be called archetypal, since it does not deny them reality but views their reality at once as anterior and posterior to, and inclusive of, any modifications they may pass through in the course of their manifestation in the relative. These empirical happenings are not unreal as far as they go, but they lack intrinsic status in their own right; they remain perforce *anattā*. This is what the loosely used word 'illusory' means in effect; things are both less and more than they seem, which is all that word is intended to convey. People often treat illusory as a virtual synonym of 'unreal', which is plainly wrong.

If a brief digression here be permissible, it is worth pointing out that the abstract concept of 'equality', supposedly applicable to mankind alone (which is already an inconsistency) and cited in justification of all manner of social and political experiments, rests on a persistent misapprehension, since it bypasses the fact that no two beings, be they human or other, can occupy a selfsame spot in 'existential space' as defined in terms of axial relationship, on which every other valuation depends. Within samsāra there is no possibility of duplication or identical repetition, hence of equality. Approximate equality is another thing, but this does not *per se* constitute a principle of value even if, empirically speaking, we ourselves are unable to discern differences which we nevertheless know must exist. Instead of ranting about equality, rather would it be true and therefore also fair to say that all beings, humans included, are born unequal and unequal must remain, a fact which spells, for each being in turn, unequal needs which, in terms of strict justice, must also call for differing means of satisfaction. In no other terms does the conception of 'natural rights' make sense.

Such is the real position; to be aware of this will make a difference to one's whole approach to problems which, admittedly, have to be dealt with in a rather rough and ready manner, often working against time. It is beyond all question that, in this ever-changing world of ours, grossly unjust situations develop from time to time, calling for redress; but reference to a pseudoprinciple of equality is not the best starting-point when trying to frame palliative policies or testing their results. The more one is able to give effect to natural inequalities, the nearer one will be to justice. Similar considerations apply to liberty: men are decidedly not born free; they are born in bondage, this being a common fate they share with all their fellow beings. Within samsaric existence, relativity, impermanence and consequent alternations of the pleasant and the painful, good and evil, remain the rule. To recognise this fact should act as a spur to compassionate effort, when such is called for, not to callous indifference – the Buddhist ethic rests on this deduction from the observed facts of life. There exist no better guidelines concerning the scope for human responsibilities than the Eightfold Path; if in the present context its two prescriptions 'proper action' and 'proper means of livelihood' are obviously the ones to heed, their relevance will assuredly be forfeited if they part company from the first item on the eightfold list, 'proper view'; this is a point which a truly Buddhist sociology must always watch. As for freedom, the call to Enlightenment is a call to achieve it: if the word *nirvāna* means a snuffing out (of ignorance) its synonym in positive form is *moksha*, deliverance. In Buddhahood itself there are no degrees; here one can properly use the word 'equality' without straining its meaning. All *Tathāgatas* have trodden a similar path (hence their title of 'suchwise come'), though the worlds to which they ministered must needs have been different. All this is worth remembering.

There is one statement which was made earlier on but which now needs qualifying, as being too bare as it stands and therefore liable to mislead if taken too literally. This is the assertion that a direct experience of the present is not possible in samsāra; it were more accurate to have said that the present is not experienceable as part of the samsaric process itself, which is a somewhat different proposition. Though an experiencing in successive mode from potential (future) to actual (past – in that order) is characteristic of that process under all circumstances, we remain as if steeped in a present we half feel and even talk about, but without really knowing what it is we are referring to. Eternity enfolds us, do or undo as we may; if it transcends us on the one hand, it is immanent and all-pervasive on the other. It would therefore be surprising if this eternal presentness did not sometimes show up on the surface of our consciousness, causing us to be wafted out of our state of more or less agitated somnambulism into that active yet calm awareness which the present bespeaks at all times. All one can say, on the strength of evidence, personal or received through others, is that such a foretasting of Enlightenment is a possibility, be it even as a rare exception, one 'that proves the rule'. But, in fact, this is not as unusual an occurrence as one might suppose; there is abundant evidence that something of the sort happens to most people on occasion, unless sophistication has blunted all their natural responsiveness as is apt to happen when a civilisation has become solidified beyond a certain point.

Those who have undergone any experience of the kind will surely recognise the signs. Suppose that a person has passed, thanks to causes one can only guess at, into a state where the ingrained habit of ratiocinative activity is temporarily in suspense, thus leaving the way clear for intuitive imagination to take charge; that person may then find himself suddenly face to face with something which, acting through the senses, will play the part of a catalyst. This thing might be a flower like the one the Buddha held up silently to Ananda with telling result; or else it might take the form of a wintry sunrise or a sudden fragrance of pines or the call of a flock of migrating geese as they pass overhead – in Tibet it would be cranes; or even in some cases an object fashioned through an exercise of human art, visual or sonorous, could serve such a purpose. Even a severe illness of the body has been known to occasion such a release from inhibiting self-consciousness, resulting in what Japanese Buddhism denotes by the word *satori*, aptly rendered by the phrase 'archetypal illumination'. It is not the exact nature of the object providing support for the bodhic ecstasy which is the decisive factor here, rather is it the man's own state of receptivity which will invite such a result.

Given that the receptive subject, by a providential conjunction of circumstances, has met his objective counterpart in one or other form, what he will then experience has the nature of a recognition, a reunion with something already familiar even before consciousness of its presence is fully aroused. Total absence of surprise is characteristic of all such meetings; all that the object does is to hold the attention of the subject gently focused, outside any consciousness the latter might have of his own selfhood. The word *anattā* is written large across every such experience.

We can then put to ourselves the question: What does the selfless beholder see or hear across this act of recollection? It is difficult to escape the conclusion that what this temporary voiding of himself enables him to perceive is the archetypal essence whereof the object that has served as a focal means of concentration is a manifested image. Let us suppose it be a rose, he will then apprehend not what a botanical dissection might lay bare but its very 'roseness' while at the same time he will see himself (not in the guise of 'ego') as presently mirrored in that same rose. The intimacy of such a state of mutual involvement goes far beyond what a merely psycho-physical appreciation could do justice to.

What can, however, be affirmed with confidence about such an encounter with archetypal reality is that it displays the character of a natural sacrament. A sacrament, to be such, implies the possibility of bringing about objective results in the animic substance of the recipient; it works *ex opere operato*, as Catholic theology has it; the mark it leaves is ineffaceable, though it may become un-recognisable under the weight of subsequent distraction and irrelevance. The same holds good for any real experience of Enlightenment, however fleeting; it stays with a man thereafter as latent knowledge, which forgetfulness may obscure but cannot efface. Mindfully cherished, such knowledge acts as a continual reminder of what it feels like to be reintegrated in one's human archetype, be it only for a few brief minutes.

The case of animals displaying an archetypal charisma is a rather special one, albeit not as rare as some might think. Usually this is brought about through contact with a human saint, but it would be rash to lay this down as an indispensable proviso; the sphere of metaphysical experience is full of paradoxical imponderables. One stirring example of such a happening in which an animal has played an essential part is mentioned in a book dating from earlier in the present century which is a classic of man's spiritual quest; this book is entitled *In search of God*, its author being Swami Ramdas, a south Indian saint who died about 1960, if I remember right. I had the privilege of meeting Swami Ramdas and obtaining from his own mouth further details of the episode in question. Piecing them all together, here is the story: During the protracted wanderings which form the subject of his book, Swami Ramdas once came upon a cave which, so he thought, would provide an ideal place for a few days' rest and meditation, so he decided to stay there, only to discover that he would have to share the cave with a large cobra whose prior right of domicile he did not fail to recognise. Nothing put off, the Swami entered the cave without the cobra seeming to mind his presence. Swami Ramdas settled down and prepared a meal, but before tasting it himself he offered some of his provisions to the cobra as *prasada*, consecrated food, which it duly consumed as if in pledge of mutual good will. Thus the two remained good neighbours for the duration of the Swami's stay until one evening, shortly before he was due to leave the cave for another place, Swami Ramdas felt moved to go outside in order to watch the setting sun, followed by the faithful reptile; while he stood there in rapturous adoration the cobra came near and coiled itself right up his leg. Soon after that they parted company; such is the story.

The way I read the evidence provided by this heart-moving tale is as follows: On meeting Swami Ramdas the cobra with unfailing instinct had recognised in him one possessing the intrinsic quality of a total human being. Moreover, such recognition automatically carried with it a restoration of the normal relationship between man and the rest of creation, a relationship ruptured, for most people, by a failure to recognise or live up to their own human vocation. This is what the teaching in the Semitic scriptures about man's 'fall from grace' implies, of which the emblematic tasting of the fruit of the dualistic tree of Good and Evil is the mythological expression. Thanks to the snake's recognition in the person of Swami Ramdas of what might be described as the 'Adamic archetype', the saint became for the cobra not only its acknowledged lord and master but also its friend and protector in an as if re-created Eden. By the same token the cobra entered into communion with its own archetype of cobrahood, for the two things hang together. Had a worldly-minded person arrived at the entrance to the cave the cobra would not have been deceived either. That the man in his state of self-deception would have murdered the animal without giving a thought is only too likely. It is the saints who really know the world and what is in it.

After this meeting with Ramdas's cobra it seems most fitting for us to meet another animal in the shape of Meister Eckhardt's flea, about which he said that 'a flea as it is in God is superior to an angel as he is in himself'. One can hardly imagine a more succinct expression of the archetypal principle than this one sentence of the greatest of Christian sages. 'A flea as it is in God' – here is the archetype of fleaness, wherein is to be found the integral reality of all that the genus *pulex*, flea, has ever covered or will cover or might cover potentially; the multitude of fleas infesting dogs or bats or sucking the blood of humans are all to be found there, not one is missing. And as for the angel 'as he is in himself', this places him among the *devas*, the 'gods of the Round' as the Tibetans designate them, who provide one of the six types of sentient beings according to the conventional classification of Buddhist cosmology. Had Meister Eckhardt spoken of an angel as he is in God, the position would have been other: the archetype of angelic existence is great indeed, but eventually no greater than any other archetype if only because, in God, greater or lesser, better or worse are terms devoid of meaning. An archetype is not 'a part of God', God is without parts. Like the divine Names or Attributes, the archetypes are one with the Divinity Itself; their plural concept comes from our side. Here I have deliberately been using a theistic phraseology to match that of Meister Eckhardt; this makes no essential difference to the argument. A similar standard of comparison applies wherever beings of any kind are to be found; it can be expressed in strictly Buddhist form if one so wishes.

One of the changes which has affected the religious climate in the West during recent times has been a steadily increasing interest in doctrines of 'non-duality' emanating for the most part from India and beyond, to which Islam has also made its contribution through the inspired teachings of the Sufi masters. A long-continued dualistic habit of viewing reality dies hard; this goes, moreover, with an excessively anthropomorphic conception of the Divine. What I have been all along trying to show, in the present essay, is how an understanding of archetypes is able to ease the intellectual passage from multiplicity to unity and back again, as between this world and what lies beyond. Here one can catch echoes of a famous phrase to be found in the *Emerald Tablet*, a work ascribed to the Graeco-Egyptian mystic who went under the name of Hermes Trismegistos. This phrase, which later became the watchword of European alchemists, can be summed up in four words: 'as below, so above'. Hermes could equally well have written: 'as here, so beyond'. This gives the gist of the question now before us.

The essential identity of *samsāra-nirvāna*, as expounded under many headings in the Mahayana sutras, remains as the paradox of paradoxes, the ultimate mystery in the face of which all attempts to specify become reduced to silence. Herein is to be seen the very archetype of mystery as such, irrespective of how the various religions may have tried to bring home this truth to their own followers. Buddhism when referring to this mystery uses for preference the word *shunyata*, Voidness, wherein every conceivable development of being is included archetypally together with every creaturely destiny; the totality of samsāra is there and so are its particularities without exception. Wherever an existential deployment may be taking place, in this world or another, this is but a rendering explicit in relative mode of what the Void carries essentially. The distinction we humans read into samsāra and nirvāna, world and voidness, itself amounts to an archetypal affirmation of relativity. As a provisional answer to metaphysical questioning such a distinction has its uses, but this does not amount to knowledge in the full sense; there is still one leap to be made, and this can only be taken in the dark. Pyrrho of Elis, founder of the Sceptic school of Greek philosophy, is credited with the remark 'we know nothing, except [the fact] that we know nothing'. Pyrrho had been to India, which at that time was something of a Mecca for Hellenic intellectuals; he had associated with those whom the Greeks called 'gymnosophists', the *nanga sannyasins* of Hinduism, but surely also with Buddhist bhikkus; in the Graeco-Bactrian kingdom which then occupied the regions now called Afghanistan, Buddhism at that time was on a rising tide and it was then that its king Menandros (indianised to 'Milinda') carried on his famous dialogue with the sage Nagasena in which the teachings about *anattā* are clearly foreshadowed. King Milinda himself became a Buddhist saint, still much venerated by the Theravadins of South East Asia. Pyrrho's warning to us is that we should not hastily conclude that we know the needful; we can be thankful for a little knowledge matched to our own intellectual limitations, but the mystery still awaits our moment of awakening, the dawn of Bodhi.

If one wishes to restate the archetypal principle in specifically Christian terms the best way to do so is by citing an actual example taken from the Gospel; it is always consonant with the Christian spirit to start out from the person of Christ himself, letting him illuminate any metaphysical questions one may have in mind. Let us then recall the occasion when Jesus, challenged by some of his hearers who felt incensed at the suggestion that such a young man might have known Abraham, made the, to them, utterly amazing reply that 'before Abraham *was*, I *am*' (John VIII verse 58) – his use of the two tenses is in itself worth a whole treatise. Despite his eminence in the line of patriarchs, Abraham was nevertheless a human being like the rest of us; he belonged to samsāra, as Buddhism would say. Christ's human nature, on the other hand, is *a priori* identified with the very archetype of humanity, he is 'True Man' as also 'Universal Man', the Transcendent Man of Taoism. Christ is also 'True God', this being the archetypal cognate of his humanity. The 'two Natures' of Christ are not just a historical coming together in time and space of the Logos, divine Word, and the man Jesus. Their archetypal association situates them together from all eternity; this is the first postulate of Christianity from which all the rest has flowed, like a stream of tradition issuing from this, its parent source. As a further deduction from this primary recognition, one can go on and say, of Creation, that it is prefigured (and post-figured) in the archetypal order. All that we now observe in the world around us or read about in history is to be found archetypally 'in God', just like Meister Eckhardt's flea. This observation, moreover, gives us a cue concerning how to understand the word 'predestination'; the great confusion that has occurred in the past between the supposedly rival claims of predestination and human free will can be blamed mostly on a false antithesis between things pertaining to two different orders of reality. Outside the archetypal order predestination makes but little sense; within it, it explains itself. Predestination corresponds in fact to God's eternal view of his own creation. By rights the prefix 'pre' might well have been omitted as being too suggestive of succession. God's view of things is always in the present and it is we who impose upon it the idea of temporality in order to accommodate it to our own worldly experience.

As for free will, this concerns man as long as he is in existence; by rights its archetype should be God's will, since this gift of free will to mankind goes with that divine image in the likeness of which man was expressly fashioned. Man's will is necessarily exercisable within the relative, but not beyond it; it cannot be opposed, even symbolically, to God's eternal willing. What a spate of verbal subtleties, of ingeniously contrived equivocations, of sophistries of every kind have been expended over the ages with a view to reconciling this free will of man's with a predestination which, seemingly, would reduce it to a cruel sham. A question badly put can never evoke a valid answer; but restate the question properly, and the answer will supply itself.

The fifth-century controversy concerning predestination and free will could be compared in certain respects to the differences, in Japanese Buddhism, between supporters of methods based respectively on *jiriki* (own power) and *tariki* (other power). Though adherents of Jodo-shin, where the latter view chiefly belongs, are apt to criticise their *jiriki* rivals for taking too much upon themselves instead of relying on Amitabha Buddha's active compassion (Christians would say, his 'grace'), neither party goes so far as to deny the quality of Buddhist orthodoxy to those from whose views they differ; rather do they admit that this a question of viewpoint and that, within the framework of a non-dualistic view of things, each interpretation will be found to imply the other, provided one looks deep enough. The same is true of the Hindu *darshanas*, or viewpoints whence to survey the Universe; those who subscribe to them may wrangle among themselves at times, but none deny to the others their legitimate place in the tradition.

It is a tragedy of Christian history that the two chief disputants in the above controversy, St Augustine and the British monk Pelagius, never managed to meet as once seemed likely. Both of them were holy men who respected one another; had such a meeting taken place this vexed question might have been brought into just perspective to the Western Church's lasting advantage; the aberrations of a Calvin might thus have been forestalled. The Eastern wing of Christianity with its richer Patristic heritage steered clear of the juridical excesses which marred so much Western theological and eschatological thinking; though even in the East the habit of unbridled invective was such as plainly called for a little Buddhist mindfulness to keep it in restraint. How many heresies became such through a premature hardening of positions brought on by partisan passion. In this respect the Indian traditions have the superior record.

To return to the question of free will, where could one find more flagrant examples of its misuse than Judas Iscariot and Devadatta, the Buddha's jealous cousin who several times tried to murder him and eventually disappeared into the earth, wreathed in flames. In terms of karma both these persons merited hell, who could doubt it? At the level of archetypes, however, such happenings have no relevance: they must be numbered among the 'accidents' of becoming and so are their karmic consequences. Had Judas and Devadatta, or Mara and Satan for that matter, awakened to the ever-present possibility of rejoining their own archetypes they could have climbed their way out of hell itself; the figure of the Buddha standing there in the midst of all the horrors is a feature of the traditional iconography which is there precisely for the purpose of bringing home this lesson. The great Sufi master 'Abd al Karim al Jili somewhere has said that hell must needs include some kind of pleasure which, by comparison with the surrounding pains, becomes a focus of attraction for the afflicted souls, thus causing them to neglect the ever-open possibility of pleading for God's mercy; did they but do so, He would surely listen. The important thing to bear in mind is that hell, any more than any other state includable in samsāra, cannot be pure horror; it cannot be pure anything, nor can a paradise of devas be so either. Purity means absence of all admixture; this is its only intrinsic meaning. The Pure Land, symbolical seat of nirvana according to Jodo-shin, is just what its name tells us; all its trees are Bodhi-trees, if one may so express oneself. Buddhism has never made the mistake of attributing 'eternity' to hell; even in Islam there is a saying to the effect that at the end of time the fires of hell will begin to cool.

One of the greatest figures of the Alexandrian school of Christian Gnosis, Origen, who suffered torture for his faith but survived and therefore technically does not rank as a martyr, was blamed by a later Church Council for suggesting that at the end of time Satan would be redeemed; no Indian-based religion would have quarrelled with such a statement. This is a case where a reference to archetypes might have obviated the conciliar censure; it is characteristic of an exoterically biased theology to take a simplistic view of a matter which, in the light of a more interior vision, would leave room for graded definitions applicable at different levels. In Buddhist mythology it is not unusual for the most malignant demons, once subdued, to submit to the Dharma and become numbered among its accredited defenders. Medieval Europe would have left them in hell for evermore and gloated over the result. Today it is the opposite that tends to happen: people often have a sneaking sympathy for the criminal exposed to the dire consequences of his misdeeds, though I would hesitate to label such a feeling as compassionate without more ado. From a Buddhist point of view an attribution of eternity to a punishment for sin however great, as also to any other relativity, betrays a metaphysical impropriety which might justly be qualified as sinful.

Turning from demons to more homely topics, it is a pleasant thought that sometimes very simple people unwittingly give utterance to an idea which from an archetypal point of view is far from foolish. Older people will doubtless remember hearing in their youth such remarks as 'When I die, what I hope for most of all is to join dear aunt Lucy; she was a real saint, never thinking of herself, never complaining, we all loved her and miss her sadly. Yes, to meet aunt Lucy, this is Heaven for me'. Nowadays, this kind of pious hope is apt to raise embarrassed smiles; mass education has tended to blunt human feeling to the point of making such naive expressions hard to take. What aunt Lucy's niece (or maybe her nephew) is saying in effect, if unconsciously, is that this much beloved aunt 'as she is in God', is certainly there waiting. The hoped-for reunion is already consummated in eternity, though for the party still living in this world it seems to lie in the future. If anyone feels minded to laugh over this example, by all means let him do so. Laughter is a divine gift, and a precious psychic safety-valve.

Enough has been said by now to show that the epithet 'eternal' is essential where archetypes are concerned. To use the latter word in regard to any phenomenon situated within the temporal order is both misleading and improper; *pace* the psychologists, relativised uses of the word 'archetype' are always best avoided. Moreover the fact that it has sometimes even been given a malefic meaning, as a cause of disintegration for the psyche under certain circumstances, shows how dangerous it is to treat it loosely. Many things which it has become usual to describe as archetypes are better rendered as 'archetypal symbols', a meaning which is both accurate and consistent.

By way of examples might be mentioned certain elementary geometrical forms such as the circle and the square, together with their solid counterparts the sphere and cube. These are archetypal symbols of primordial efficacy, to which might be added the equilateral triangle, which when combined with an inversion of itself gives us the seal of Solomon, cardinal emblem of the Jewish tradition but also used in many other connections.

The Cross is of course a major archetypal symbol whose components, vertical and horizontal, between them span the Universe; this subject has already been touched on when describing the three-dimensional mandala. Certain numbers also have belonged to this superior category of symbols, from the time of Pythagoras onward; no need to list them here. In the plant world we have the lotus, rose and shamrock; among animals we have the eagle – the 'thunderbird' of Amerindian tradition – the sacred cow of Hinduism and two Christian animals, namely the Dove standing for Spirit and the downflow of Grace, and the Lamb referable to the archetype of sacrifice. There is no end to such examples which between them go to form a kind of archetypal Algebra, of which the supreme equation is expressed in terms of *alpha* and *omega*, beginning and end with all their intermediate implications.

Such archetypal symbols have been a mainstay of traditional art from primitive times until now; many of the major forms of art rest on a geometric basis into which other, more topical symbols may be fitted in their turn. The medieval cathedrals are a well-known case which has attracted much attention in recent years, thanks to the work of some architectural investigators of unusual perspicacity. The Tibetan form of mandala, to be seen both on the walls of temples and on painted scrolls, uses a framework consisting of a circle with a square inscribed in it; the phrase 'squaring the circle' may be recalled in this connection. Given this framework, other related details will be fitted in, in the form of ritual objects, such as the *vajra* and bell representing method and wisdom, angelic attendants with their appropriate colours, and so on. Occupying the centre of the mandala one finds a presiding figure in the form of a Buddha, Bodhisattva or other celestial portrait; such a scheme is always associated with a given course of meditation, to be carried out under guidance by one's lama; the mandala's purpose is to serve as a mnemonic aid for the disciple undergoing instruction. So much for the legitimate use of symbols; anti-symbols, created through a deliberate reversing of known archetypal forms, are the hallmark of black sorcery the world over.

A special word needs saying about the Chinese and Japanese art of landscape as a spiritual support of near-miraculous potency. There is no doubt that the Far Eastern artists exercised their skill with a conscious intention of revealing essences; merely aesthetic motives entered neither into their training nor their practice. It is characteristic of this style of landscape that it seems to separate almost imperceptibly from the Void only to sink back there, after a deployment that never exceeds the necessary, as mysteriously as when it first emerged; it is sometimes hard to believe that brush and paint have played a part in producing such a result. Anyone who has lived close to one of these paintings will bear witness to its unique power to attract attention whenever one comes within range of it; call this an art or a science, it certainly partakes of both. Two traditions, the Taoist and the Buddhist, have converged in producing what can without exaggeration be given the name of 'archetypal art'. In other styles of painting one may come across examples that display a similar quality by exception; but it is only in the Far East that this became almost the rule so long, that is to say as the tradition itself remained unbroken.

Before closing the present far-flung discussion it is worth remarking that a being will normally participate in several archetypes at once; when one speaks of an individual archetype one means as a rule a synthesis of all such interwoven strands of archetypal influence as have converged, at this world's level (failing which the word 'several' could not apply), into determining that being's vocation, its *svadharma*; here one's karma, the fruits of a relative free will, and one's dharma, archetypal predestination, coincide in fact.

But enough of details! This discussion has led us far afield; it seems high time for us to be going home. What then is 'home' in the context of this essay?

Uniting with one's archetype, this is what home means for every being that ever was; *moksha*, deliverance means nothing else. The land of archetypes is the Pure Land. The Greek Fathers from quite early times had a word for this repatriation; they called it 'deification', a highly paradoxical word to use since how, it may be asked, can a created being think of becoming God? 'How' is the key-word here; uniting with one's archetype is but to rejoin that which one already is 'in God', to quote Meister Eckhardt's phrase once again. The essential 'non-duality' of samsāra and nirvana is our proof that such is possible once that arch-prodigal, the samsaric wanderer, has made tracks for the parental home where the dreary cycle of birth and death may once and for all be ended.

Of all things proceeding from a cause, the cause has been shown by Him-thus-come and also their cessation, the great Mendicant has declared. So speaks the Vinaya-pitaka, Mahāvagga I, 23. The message of the archetypes is but speaking the same hope.